# THE YALPANA-VAIPAVA-MALAI
# OR
# THE HISTORY OF THE KINGDOM OF JAFFNA

# THE YALPANA-VAIPAVA-MALAI
# OR
# THE HISTORY OF THE KINGDOM OF JAFFNA

TRANSLATED FROM THE TAMIL
WITH AN APPENDIX AND A GLOSSARY

C. BRITO

GYAN

*Published by*

GYAN

Gyan Publishing House
5, Ansari Road
Daryaganj, New Delhi-110002
Phone: 011-47034999, 9811692060
E-mail: books@gyanbooks.com

*Distribution Network*
gyanbooks.com
India, USA, Canada, UK, Australia, France



ISBN : 978-81-212-4233-2 (PB)
First Published, Colombo, 1879

2nd Impression 2020

*Printed at:* Gyan Press, Delhi.



**The Yalpana-Vaipava-Malai or The History of the Kingdom of Jaffna**
Author: C. Brito

THE

# YALPANA-VAIPAVA-MALAI

OR

THE HISTORY OF THE KINGDOM OF JAFFNA,

TRANSLATED FROM THE TAMIL,

WITH

AN APPENDIX AND A GLOSSARY,

BY

C. BRITO.

COLOMBO:

1879.

TO

THE MEMORY OF

PERCIVAL ACKLAND DYKE, ESQ.

WHO,

DURING HIS

LONG, WISE AND UPRIGHT ADMINISTRATION,

AS GOVERNMENT AGENT OF THE NORTHERN PROVINCE,

WHILE MAINTAINING THE MUNIFICENCE AND SPLENDOUR

OF AN EASTERN PRINCE,

CONFERRED

ON WHAT HAD ONCE BEEN THE ANCIENT KINGDOM OF JAFFNA

'HOSE BLESSINGS OF PEACE AND HAPPINESS,

WHICH IT HAD NEVER BEFORE, NOR HAS EVER SINCE

ENJOYED,

THIS BOOK IS HUMBLY

DEDICATED

# CONTENTS.

## THE AUTHOR'S PREFACE.

At the request of the illustrious Dutch Governor Maccara, this work, in Tamil prose, was undertaken by Mayilvakanan, a descendant of the celebrated Vaiya, the uthor of the poem "Para-rasa-sekeran-ula" and the chronicle "Rasa-murai", made in the reign of king Seka-rasa-sekaran, out of materials collected from "the Kayilasa-malai" and other ancient works.

# THE TRANSLATOR'S PREFACE.

This is a free translation, but it preserves, to a great extent, the modes of thought and expression peculiar to the Tamil original.

In the transliteration of foreign names into English, the translator has not been able to follow any method. The same name is differently spelt and pronounced by different writers, according as they adopt the Tamil, Singhalese, or Sanscrit form.

All that is known of the author is what he says of himself in his preface. The Governor Maccara, of whom he speaks, was Jan Maccara who was Governor of the Dutch possessions of Ceylon in 1736. And there is sufficient internal evidence to shew that the author lived about that time, but the bold language in which the policy of the Dutch is described and the prophecies which the work contains, relating to the English, must be regarded as interpolations of a later date.

The work is looked upon as one of great authority among the Tamils of Jaffna, and there are several manuscript copies of it extant in the peninsula.

The Appendix and the Glossary which are added to this translation will, it is hoped, be found useful not merely towards a right understanding of the author, but as explaining points of general interest connected with the history and literature of the Island.

Colombo,

July 10th, 1879.

# The Yalpana Vaipava Malai.

IT is related in the *ithihasas* and *puranas* that the *Rakshasas* held *Langka* during the first three *yugas* of the world. Tradition adds that *Vibhishana*, who received the kingdom from *Dasarata Rama*, the conqueror of *Ravana*, continued to reign up to and during the early part of the present *yuga*, and that when *Vibhishana* was taken up to heaven, the *Rakshasas* quitted *Langka* from fear of foreign subjugation. The Rakshasas.

About two thousand four hundred years ago, *Singhabahu* a *Kshattriya* of *Banga* was king of *Lada*. His eldest son, *Vijaya-kumara*, a lawless youth, rendered himself extremely hateful to his countrymen, and was in consequence expelled the kingdom. The exile wandered from place to place in search of an asylum, but he found none. Singha-bahu. Vijaya.

When at last he reached *Kashi* he was informed in a dream that *Langka* was assigned to him for a heritage, and that he should go thither and establish himself at *Kathirai-malai* in the centre of the country. He went accordingly, and took with him, besides his usual retinue, a priest of the name of *Nilakanda-acharya*, a *Brahman* of *Kashi*. The *Brahman* was accompanied by his whole The acharya.

family, which consisted of his wife, *Akilanda-valli-ammal*, and his sons and daughters with their wives and husbands. The expedition safely reached its destination, and advancing into the heart of the country took up its residence at *Kathirai-malai*.

Vedar.

In those days *Langka* was a great wilderness, inhabited only by the *Vedar* and wild animals. There were no human beings in it. And *Vijaya-raja* (for *raja* i. e. *king* he now undoubtedly was) made constant efforts to obtain colonists from the adjacent countries. From *Kanya-kumari* to the *Himalaya* mountains, all despised "the country of the *Rakshasas*", as they termed *Langka* in contempt. The baffled king turned his thoughts to the *Buddhists* of *Magadha*, who had been driven from their country by reason of their having embraced *Buddhism*. Some of them had already found permanent seats in the countries lying to the North of the *Himalaya* mountains; but others, who had travelled eastward and crossed the *Brahmaputtra*, were as yet leading a wandering life in *Siam* and other parts of *Burma*. *Vijaya-raja* went to *Siam*, and successfully induced a number of those wanderers to follow him into the new kingdom. He placed them in various parts of the country, and gave them liberty to follow their own faith. In process of time these *Buddhists* came to be called *Singhalese* from the fact of their inhabiting *Singhalam*.—"*Singhalam*" being another name for "*Langka*."

First colony.

*Vijaya-raja* did not himself profess *Buddhism*, but he only tolerated it as a means of peopling the country. He was a staunch worshipper of *Siva*: and began his reign by dedicating his city to that god and building four *Sivalayams* as a protection for the four quarters of his infant kingdom:—In the East he erected *Konesar-koyil* at *Thampala-kamam*: In the West he re-built *Thiruk-kethich-churan-koyil*, which had long been then in ruins: In the South he raised *Santhira-sekaran-koyil* at *Mathlthurai*: and on the North he constructed *Thiruth-thampa-lesuran-koyil* and *Thiruth-thampa-lesuvari-amman-koyil* at *Thiruth-thampalai*, at the foot of *Kiri-malai*. Near the last mentioned two *koyils* he caused a third to be built which he dedicated to *Kathirai-andavar*. Over these three temples he appointed *Vamatheva-acharya*, the third son of the *Kashi-brahman*, *Nila-kanda-acharya*, to be priest, and assigned to him and his wife, *Visalakshi-ammal*, a habitation in the neighbourhood, which he had carefully supplied with everything necessary for their comfort. From the circumstance of there being three *koyils* at *Thiruth-thampalai* its name was changed into *Koyil-kadavai*. The four temples.

*Koyil-kadavai* was the scene of the meditations and austerities of *Nakula-muni*, a holy sage, who lived in a cave at the foot of *Nakula-malai*, a hill so called after him. *Nakulam* means a *mongoose*, and the *muni* was so named from the resemblance which his face bore to that of a mongoose. Of this deformity the *muni* was subsequently Nakulamuni.

cured in a miraculous manner; for, it disappeared when he bathed in the waters of the streamlet which issues from the hill and discharges itself into the sea. *Nakula-malai* is frequenly known by the name of *Kiri-malai*, from *kiri*, which is another word for mongoose. In honour of this *muni*, who was constantly found performing religious duties in *Thiruth-thampa-lesuvaran-koyil* and *Thiruth-thampa-lesuvari-amman-koyil*, posterity has changed the names of these temples into *Naku-lesar-koyil* and *Naku-lampikai-amman-koyil* respectively.

After the building of the temples, *Vijaya-raja* returned to *Kathirai-malai* making a circuit of the whole country. On reaching his capital he removed the seat of government to *Thammanna*:—a change which was followed by another and a cruel one, for he drove away his wife with her two children, a son and a daughter, whom she had borne to him, and took another wife in the person of a woman from *Pandi*.

Death of Vijaya.

*Vijaya-raja* reigned but a few years after this. He left no issue, and his minister took charge of the kingdom and preserved it for a year, until the arrival of the late king's brother's son, *Pandu-vasu*, whom the minister had sent for from *Lada*. This *Pandu-vasu* was the founder of an illustrious dynasty which continued to reign over *Langka* for numerous generations.

Arrival of Kulak-koddan.

In the year 358 of the *Salivakana-sakaptham*, *Kulak-koddu-maha-raja*, son of *Manu-nithi-kanda-cholan* of *Kave-*

*rip-pum-paddanam*, set out on a pilgrimage to sacred places. At *Thiri-kona-malai* he visited *Konesar-koyil*, and, learning that the *Sivalayam, Konesar-koyil*, at *Thampala-kamam* was falling into ruin, he went thither and busied himself in repairing it and the buildings attached to it.

The reign of Pandu.

*Pandu-maha-raja* who ruled *Langka* from *Anuradhapura*, was at this time absent from his capital, having come to *Manat-tidal* (the sand-heap), a name by which this part of his kingdom was then known. The inhabitants of *Koyil-kadavai* seized the opportunity to complain to the king against certain *Singhalese* traders in that district, who supplied dried fish to foreign markets. The complaint was that they exposed fish to dry in holy places and polluted holy wells by drawing water from them, and that, therefore, priests and devotees felt constrained to abandon the temples. *Pandu* inquired into the matter and punished the offenders according to justice. Finding that the *Singhalese* themselves did not know how to fish, but that they employed for the purpose labourers of the *Mukkuva* caste—a caste whose hereditary occupation fishing was—the king ordered every individual of the *Mukkuva* caste to quit the sacred neighbourhood. The *Mukkuva* chieftains, *Usuman* and *Senthan*, migrated with their followers to *Batticaloa* and settled in *Panakai* and *Valaiyiravu*. A few remained behind in *Manat-tidal*, but formed new settlements on the sea coast far removed from *Kiri-malai*. From this time

The mukkuvar

no *Mukkuvar* have been found in *Usuman-thurai*, *Senthan-kalam* or *Allith-thundal.*

Kulak-koddan. While *Pandu* was thus engaged here, his queen at *Anuradhapura* received information of the doings of *Kulak-koddan*, and despatched a small army with instructions to drive him out of the kingdom. When the army reached *Thampala-kamam* and witnessed the gigantic undertakings of the enemy, it trembled with fear, and approaching *Kulak-koddan* represented itself to have come to him on a pacific mission, having been sent by the court of *Anuradhapura* only to inquire if he needed any assistance. *Kulak-koddan* affected to believe the representation, received the soldiers with apparent kindness, entertained them sumptuously, and dismissed them with valuable presents and a friendly reply to their mistress. On their return to *Anuradhapura* they published such exaggerated accounts of the stranger's greatness and liberality, that no attempt was ever afterwards made to molest him in his career.

As soon as *Kulak-koddan* had completed the buildings, he prepared seven large tracts of land with fruitful groves and fertile fields, and dedicated their income for the

The Vanniyar. use of the temple. He sent for *Vanniyar* from the coast of India, and placed them over those tracts, with strict orders to them to cultivate the lands for the benefit of the temple.

At first, the income of these lands was regularly delivered, and was amply sufficient for the expenses of the temple, the monasteries and the *akkiraram*; and these institutions, accordingly, flourished. On the death of *Kulak-koddan* (which took place in his native country after his return from *Langka)*, the *Vanniyar*, who had rapidly increased in number, and had besides received an accession of fifty-nine new families from *Pandi*, became too numerous to be capable of attending to their lands peacefully without a king. They began to fight with one another for supremacy, and the cultivation of the lands was necessarily neglected. A host of ephemeral kings rose and disappeared in succession. The most distinguished of them was *Santhira-vanniyan.* He, too, fell in the internecine contest, but the survivors continued the fight till they were all exhausted. A peace was, at length, concluded, and seven chieftains were elected from among the *Vanniyar* to exercise sovereign power, each within his own territory. The descendants of these chieftains continued to exercise the like power, and the territories over which they ruled came to be called the *Vannis*, i.e. the territories of the *Vanniyar*.

In the year 515 of the *Salivakana-sakaptham*, *Aggra-bhodi-maha-raja* perceived that the then reigning *Vanniyar* were elated with pride and fancied themselves to be independent kings. He, therefore, reduced them to their true position, namely that of *athikaries*—a position which they ever afterwards retained. Before this time the sovereigns of *Anuradhapura* had taken no notice of the *Vannis*, inasmuch as all the revenue of those districts went to the temple as appointed by *Kulakkoddan*.

Ukkirasingkan.

In the year 717 of the *Salivakana-sakaptham*, *Ukkira singkan*, a prince of the dynasty founded by king *Vijaya's* brother, made a descent upon *Langka* with a numerous force from the *Vada-thesam* (the northern country, i.e India), and after a severe struggle possessed himself of one half of *Langka*, which had been lost to the dynasty for a long time. He reigned from *Kathirai-malai*, while another king ruled over the Southern territories.

This *Ukkira-singka-maha-rasan's* face was like that of a lion. Having been assured that he would be cured of the deformity if he made a pilgrimage to *Nakulesar-koyil*, he went to *Kiri-malai* and pitched his tent in *Valavar-kon-pallam*, a valley so named from *Valavan* (*Chola-rasan*), who had formerly encamped on the same spot when he too had come out on a pilgrimage to this sacred place.

Thondaman's visit.

It was when *Ukkira-singkan* was encamped here, that he received a visit from the *Thondaman*, king of *Thondai-nadu*, who landed near *Kiri-malai* and came with a numerous retinue to meet the king, in order to ask permission to buy salt from the inhabitants of *Karanavai*, *Vellappara-vai*, and other places where salt was usually found, and, for that purpose, to open a passage so as to admit of his vessels being taken from the northern sea to the salt pans. The *Thondaman* got all the privileges he applied for. A small, shallow channel, which he caused to be deepened and widened in the exercise of his privileges, forms the majestic canal which we now call the *Thondaman-aru.* In connection with this canal, the *Thondaman* caused also an inland harbour to be dug, in order to give shelter to his vessels during the monsoons.

**Thondaman-aru.**

Returning from *Kiri-malai Ukkira-singkan* passed through the *Vannis,* received the voluntary submission of the seven *Vanniyar,* and imposed a tribute upon them, which, he enjoined, should be paid to the temple of *Konesar,* as had been done by their predecessors.

**Submission of the Vanniyar.**

About eight years after these events, a daughter of king *Thisai-yukkira-cholan* of *Chola-thesàm,* of the name of *Maruthap-pira-vika-valli,* who had an equine face and an emaciated form caused by a painful gripe that had baffled all human attempts at cure, came to *Kiri-malai,* having heard of its great sanctity through an ascetic of the name of *Santha-lingkan.* The place where she was encamped has been called after her, *Kumaraththi-pallam,* i. e. the Princess' valley. By direction of *Nakula-muni,* who did not fail to give her an account of his own cure and the holiness of the place, she bathed in the sea at the spot where the sea receives the *Kiri-malai* stream and preserves its freshness in the midst of salt water :—a spot more holy than all other sacred places in the world.

**Maruthap-pira-vika-valli.**

Here she remained a considerable time repeating her prayers and ablutions daily until the miraculous waves washed away her deformity and pain, and transformed her into a marvel of beauty. A change in the name of the place preserves the memory of this event, for *Koyil-kadavai* has given place to *Ma-vidda-puram* [*ma=horse, vidda=left off, puram=place.*]

Ma-vidda-puram.

Kantha-suvami-koil built.

*Maruthap-pira-vika-valli* wished to build a temple to *Kantha-suvami* at the scene of her recovery. At her request, her father *Thisai-yukkira-cholan* supplied her with the men and materials required for so great an undertaking. There was one requisite, however, that even royalty could not easily supply, namely a *Brahman* for performing sacred rites, as it is accounted a great pollution for *Brahmans* to cross the sea or dwell in the land of the *Rakshasas.* When promises and persuasion were found ineffectual, the king sent a message to the chief of the three thousand *Brahmans* of the *Sivalayam* at *Thillai*, peremptorily ordering him to find one among the number that would go to *Langka*. Astounded at the strange demand the chief shut himself up in the *alayam*, resolving to starve himself there to death, rather than force one of his number to lose caste and heaven by obeying the king. On the third day of his abstinence he was favoured with a vision which revealed to him the sanctity of *Kiri-malai*, the presence of *Nakula-muni* there, and the shortness of the voyage that would be vouchsafed to the passenger so as to enable him to perform the morning rites on the *Indian* shore, and the evening rites on the other. Thus miraculously encouraged one *Periya-manath-thullar* consented to go to *Langka.* The king entrusted him with the transport of the images of *Kantha-suvami, Valli-yamman* and *Theyva-nayaki-yamman,* besides a lot of utensils and furniture for the use of the temple. With these he landed at *Kasath-thurai* now called *Kangkesan-thurai* from the fact of the landing of the image of *Kangkeyan* (another name for *Kantha-suvami.*)

Arrival of Periya-manath-thullar in Langka.

About this time *Ukkira-singka-maha-rasa* made his third visit to *Manat-tidal,* and, being struck with the beauty of *Maruthap-pira-vika-valli,* whom he met at *Kiri-malai,* he entered her apartments in the middle of the night as she lay awake in bed thinking of the temple she was building, and boldly carried her away through the lines of her guards and soldiers. Her maids and attendants were greatly distressed at the disappearance of their mistress, but were comforted on learning that *Ukkira-singka-maha-rasa* had made her his queen. And they immediately returned home to *Chola-nadu* carrying the happy news to her parents, the king having liberally provided them with everything necessary for the voyage. In deference to the wishes of *Maruthap-pira-vika-valli,* the king remained here until she had completed the temple, and witnessed the *thusarokanam* (hoisting of the flag) of the first festival, which took place in the month of *Ani,* under the asterism *Uththiram.* He then carried her to *Kathirai-malai,* celebrated the nuptial ceremonies with great pomp,

Maruthap-pira-vika-valli married to Ukkira-singka-maha-rasa.

and lived long on earth enjoying the married happiness of *Indra* and *Indrani* in heaven.

Periya-manath-thullar's marriage.

It is a fact that has carried proverbial notoriety that the ladies of the district of *Thillai* never step beyond the limits of their district. As a result of this prejudice *Periya-manath-thullar* failed to get a wife from among his own relatives. He therefore looked for one among strangers and selected the daughter of *Sampa-siva-ayyar* of the *Kashi* race. Her name was *Valampen*, which, after her marriage, she changed into *Thillai-navaka-valli* in order to please her husband who retained a great fondness for this native *Thillai*. With this wife he lived in happiness in an *akkiraram* to the south of the temple and performed his duties regularly. In the offspring of this union the *Kashi* and the *Thillai* races of priesthood became united and both houses ever afterwards acknowledged but one common head.

Birth of Nara-singka-rasa and Senpaka-vathi.

Soon after his return from *Manat-tidal*, *Ukkira-singka-maha-rasan* abandoned *Kathirai-malai* and made *Senkada-ka-nakari* his capital. In the new capital the queen gave birth to two children, first a son, and then a daughter. The former was beautiful as *Manmathan* (the god of love) and had all the marks of royalty, with the tail of a lion besides. He was named *Nara-singka-rasa* and his sister *Senpaka-vathi*. Their parents united them in marriage and crowned the son sub-king with the title of *Vala-singka-rasa*, but on his father's death he ascended the throne under the title of *Jeya-thungka-vara-rasa-singkan.*

It was in the reign of *Jeya-thungka-vara-rasa-singkan* that the blind poet *Vira-rakavan* came from *Chola-thesam* to *Langka.* At *Sengkadaka-nakari* he recited a poem of great merit which he had composed in praise of the king; but he pleased the king more by his performance on the lyre, and was rewarded for his skill with the sovereignty of this the northern part of *Langka* then called *Manat-tidal,* a name which has since been superseded by that of *Yalpanam,* from *yal* a *lyre,* and *panan* a poet. The Yalpanan assumed the state and responsibilities incidental to the new dignity: he got out several *Tamil* colonists from the *Vada-thesam* (the northern country, i. e. Southern India) and planted them in various parts of the kingdom. These new colonists and the *Singhalese* natives he treated alike, and, after a long and prosperous reign, died of old age. He left no issue to succeed him, and there arose violent disturbances among his subjects: the *Singhalese* and the *Tamils* were jealous of each other and fought for supremacy. In this state of the country a great many *Tamil* families thought it prudent to return to India. Vira-rakavan. Yalpanam.

But there was one *Tamil* colonist, a nobleman of the name of *Malavan,* a *Velalen* of *Ponpatti-yur* in *Pandi-nadu,* who remained here during the troublous times and successfully opposed the *Singhalese.* Hearing that a prince Malavan.

of the *Chola* dynasty, a nephew of *Singka-kethu*, the son of *Thisai-yukkira-cholan* had left his home in *Chola-nadu* and was then residing at *Mathurai*, prosecuting such studies in the college there as became his royal birth, *Malavan* went thither and prevailed upon him to go over and take possession of the vacant throne. This prince's name was *Singka-ariyan*. From a defect in one of his arms he was known in his early days by the nickname

Kulang-kayan

of *Kulang-kayan* i. e. "the short-handed," and has afterwards been celebrated in the pages of history by those of *Kulang-kai-ariyan* and *Visaya-kulang-kaich-chakkira-varththi*. He set out with his minister the far-famed *Puvineka-vaku* and a priest of the name of *Kangkathara-ayyar*, a *Brahman* of the *Kashi* race. The good wishes of the *Pandiyan* and a large army raised under his auspices followed the young prince to *Yalpanam*. Landing on the shores of his future kingdom he advanced into the country without any opposition and pitched his camp on the plains, on which he afterwards built the city of

Nallur.

*Nallur* with all its ramparts, gates, mansions, palaces, towers, flower-gardens, baths, stables for elephants and horses, halls of justice, pleasure-houses, dwellings for *Brahmans* and warriors, and an *akkiraram* for *Kangkatha-rar* and his wife *Anna-purani-ammal*. He dug a three-sided well with whose water, he mixed water brought from the sacred river *Yamunai*. He built temples on all the four sides of his city. On the east *Veyiluvan-*

*thappillaiyar-koyil*, on the west *Viramakali-amman-koyil*, on the south *Kayilai-vinayakar-koyil*, and on the north the *Koyils* of *Sadda-nath-esuran*, *Thaiyal-nayaki-amman* and *Salai-vinayakar*. He made a public entry into the new city with his queen *Thilaka-vathiyar* under happy omens and benignant stars, and celebrated the occasion with great joy and splendour.

At the advice of his minister he wrote to the kings of *Tamil* countries requesting them to send him colonists. Accordingly a number of families came over attended with all their slaves and dependants. The settlements assigned to the principal colonists are as follows :— The new colonists and their settlements.

*Malavan* (a *Velalan* from *Ponpatti-yur* in *Pandi*), his brother, his cousin *Sanpaka Malavan*, and another cousin of his were placed at *Thirunelveli*.

*Nara-singka-thevan*, the eldest son of *Puravalanthi Thevan* from *Kaviri-yur* at *Mayiliddi*.

*Senpaka Mappanan*, a *Velalan* from *Vavikka*, his relative *Santhira-sekara Mappanan*, *Puppanan of Kayilnakar* a *Velalan* and *Kanakarayan* a *Cheddi*, at *Thellippalai*.

*Perayira-mudaiyan* from *Kovalur* a *Velalan*, at *Inuvil*. This colonist afterwards abandoned *Inuvil* as it was an uncultivated place and went and settled towards the north of it.

*Nilakandan* a *Velalan* from *Kachchur*, distinguished by many royal favours, and his four brothers, at *Pachchilaippalli*.

*Kanaka-puvan* (or *Kanaka-Malavan*) a *Velulan* from *Sikarama-nakar* and his four brothers, at *Puloli.*

*Kupaka-rayenthiran* a *Velalan* from *Kupanadu*, and *Punniya-pupalan*, at *Tholpuram.*

*Theva-rayenthiran* of *Puththur* a *Velalan*, at *Koyilakkandi.*

*Mannadu konda Muthali* of *Thondai-mandalam*, of the very high *Velala* family in honor of which the poem *Erelupathu* of poet *Kampan* was made, at *Irumanai* or *Irupalai.*

*Irumarapum-thuyya Thaninayakan* of *Seyyur*, at *Nedunthivu.*

*Pallavan*, a nobleman of *Vagnchi-nakar* and two other noblemen, at *Velinadu* now called *Pallavarayan-kaddu.*

The king appointed four veteran heroes as *athikarikal* of the four quarters of his kingdom:—namely, the valiant *Valliya-mathakkan* on the west, the matchless *Imaiyana-mathakkan* on the north, the warlike *Senpaka-mathakkan* on the east, and the brave *Vetti-mathakkan* on the south.

The command of the forces was given to *Virasingkan*, a prince of warriors.

After these arrangements for the safety and government of the kingdom, the king caused himself to be crowned on an auspicious day and at a happy conjunction of the planets. He led a magnificent procession through the city and ascended his throne like an *Indra* on earth and reigned in undisturbed peace and happiness.

Nallur Temple.

By direction of the king, *Puvineya Vaku* commenced to build the temple of *Kantha-suvami* at *Nallur*, which, with its outer walls and towers, he finished in the year 870 of the *Salivakana sakaptham.*

King's visit to Kiri-malai.

The same year the king and his minister made a visit to *Kiri-malai* to wash themselves in the sacred waters, and to worship at the temples; which when they had done, their attention having been directed to the state of the edifices, they placed the temples and their revenues under the supervision of the king's officers.

Feast.

*Sinna-manath-thullar* son of *Sithampara-thidehathar* and grandson of *Periya-manath-thullar* was then priest of *Kantha-Suvami-koyil*, and he entertained the king and his retinue at a grand feast which he gave in honor of the occasion. The minister who was one of the best *Tamil* scholars of the age was tempted to extemporize a stanza at each of the varieties of food placed before the guests. To give an idea of the sentiments which those stanzas contained one specimen must suffice.

"The food given by *Sinna-manath-thullar* can only be compared with the *Amirtha* which *Vishnu* gave to the gods in times gone by. Had the gods but had a taste of *Sinna-manath-thullar's* feast they had never given themselves the trouble of churning the Ocean."

One night, as the king lay asleep in his *Sappira-mugncham*, *Paramesvaran* and *Parvathi* appeared to him in a dream. In compliance with the divine commission

Building of a new Temple at Nallur

then revealed to him, he built a temple for *Kayilaya-nathar* and *Kayilai-nayaki-amman*, and embellished it above all other temples. He added to it three halls for displaying the divine image, one hall for the attendant gods, besides granaries, almshouses, *akkiraram*, streets for cars, monasteries, halting houses for travellers and other like establishments. He surrounded the whole with walls and towers of due proportion. He sent for the *lingam* which *Manmathan* worshipped at *Ketharam* and placed it in the new temple. *Sethupathi*, the chief of *Iramanathapuram* and first captain of the forces of the king of *Pandi* procured for him a *Brahman* from *Kashi* whose name was *Kangkathara-ayyar*. Having appointed *Kangkathara-ayyar* priest of the new temple, and, worshipping therein the god *Kayilasa-nathar* day and night, long did the king reign over this kingdom of *Yalpanam* from the city of *Nallur*, a *Kayilasam* on earth.

Kula-sekara-singkai-ariyan

When this king died he was succeeded by his son *Kula-sekara-singkai-ariyan* a pacific prince who effected reforms in the administration of the government, and increased his own revenue together with the happiness of his subjects by promoting agriculture.

Kuloth-thungka-sinkai-ariyan.

*Kula-sekara-singkai-ariyan* was succeeded by his son *Kuloth-thungka-singkai-ariyan*, who, following in the footsteps of his excellent father, helped his subjects to bring waste land into cultivation and thereby contributed to their happiness and the increase of his own revenue.

In this reign there reigned peace and tranquillity throughout the whole kingdom.

But on the occasion of his son *Vikkirama-singkai-ariya* coming to the throne, a great disturbance arose between the *Singhalese* of this place who were *Buddhists,* and the *Tamils,* in matters connected with religion. In an affray between the factions two *Tamils* were killed and a few wounded. The king inquired into the matter and executed *Pugnchi-Banda,* the ring leader of the *Singhalese,* with seventeen of his followers and punished the rest of the offenders with imprisonment. Many of the *Singhalese* fled from the country, while those that remained behind cherished an intense hatred of the king on account of his partiality to the *Tamils* and made him spend the rest of his life in constant dread of plots and insurrections. He died in the midst of his anxieties and was succeeded by his son *Varothaya-singkai-ariyan.*

**Vikkirama-singkai-ariyan**

**Religious squabble.**

*Varothaya-singkai-ariyan* was a wise sovereign. He made regulations concerning the matters of religion which caused the disturbance in the late reign ; he restrained all classes within their proper limits and quieted the animosities of the contending factions. At his death he left a peaceful kingdom to his son, *Maththanda-singkai-ariyan.*

**Varothaya-singkai ariyan**

*Math-thanda-singkai-ariyan's* reign was however disturbed by an insurrection among his subjects, which

**Math-thanda-singkai-ariyan**

was fomented by the jealousy of the *Vanniyar.* The king quelled it without any difficulty and devoted the rest of his reign to the promotion of education and agriculture. He was a just and humane ruler and died sincerely regretted by both factions of his subjects.

Kunapushana-singkai-ariyan

His son and successor *Kuna-pushana-singkai-ariyan* was even more successful than his father in winning the affections of the people. He treated all his subjects alike, rendered his rule firm and promoted education and industry throughout his long reign. Weighed down with extreme old age he felt himself unequal to the burden of a kingdom and he accordingly abdicated it in favor of his son *Virothaya-singkai-ariyan.*

Virothaya-singkai-ariyan

The reign of *Virothaya-singkai-ariyan* was an eventful one. The *Vanniyar* kept constantly inciting the *Singhalese* to insurrection, which gave him constant employment in the field. He put down every insurrection with energy, and he wished to be revenged on the *Vanniyar.* He marched against them with a well appointed army,

Invasion of the Vannis.

routed them in every battle, gave up the *Vannis* to rapine and plunder, and rendered them utterly powerless. The fate of the *Vanniyar* had a salutary effect on the minds of the disaffected *Singhalese*: they quietly returned to their duty and falling at the feet of the king implored forgiveness for their past offences. The king readily gave it to them and treated them ever afterwards with as much kindness as if they had never revolted.

It was in this reign that *Santhira-sekara Pandiyan*, king of *Mathurai*, driven from his kingdom by foreign invasion wandered into *Ilangkai* in search of an asylum. *Virothaya-singkai-ariyan* befriended the fallen monarch, brought together his scattered army, added to it a numerous force of his own, crossed the sea, beseiged *Mathurai*, fought many bloody engagements, routed the usurpers and reinstated the *Pandiyan* on his throne.

Invasion of Mathurai.

While the king was occupied on the continent, the restless *Vanniyar* were anxious to profit by his absence. They affected to believe that he designed to sack the *Vannis* again, and, on this pretext, they implored the assistance of the court of *Kandi* to invade his territories. But the *Kandiyan* king declined to violate, as he put it, the sanctity of the grant which one of his ancestors had made to the blind poet. To the disappointed *Vanniyar* there was but one way of safety open, and of that they did not fail to avail themselves. They waited upon *Virothaya-singkai-ariyan* on his return and appeased his just resentment with large presents and by their humble behaviour.

Disaffection of the Vanniyar.

This king died young and the cause of his death has never been ascertained. He took his evening meal as usual and went to sleep apparently in good health, but was next morning found dead in his bed. There was a wide spread suspicion which attributed the death to foul play.

Jeyavira-singkai-ariyan.

His eldest son *Jeya-vira-singkai-ariyan* was a mere boy when he mounted his father's throne, but he ruled the kingdom with consummate wisdom, and protected his subjects from foreign and domestic foes.

War with the king of Kandi.

In the year 1380 of the *Salivakana Sakapatham* this celebrated young king had a misunderstanding with *Puvineya-vaku*, king of *Kandi*, touching the pearl fishery. Both kings rushed to arms, and after severe losses on both sides victory declared herself in favour of *Jeya-vira-singkai-ariyan*. The victor became master of the territories of the vanquished, and one flag, the flag of *Yalpanam* (*Gemini* holding a lyre), waved over the whole *Ilangkai*. This state of things continued for twelve years, when the king of *Yalpanam* restored the kingdom of *Kandi* to king *Parakkirama Vaku* on his undertaking to pay a tribute. This amicable arrangement was brought about by the interference of the *Pandiyan* who personally guaranteed the due payment of the tribute by the king of *Kandi*. And *Kandi* continued to be a tributary of this kingdom for a number of successive reigns.

Kunavira-singkai-ariyan.

*Jeya-vira-singkai-ariyan* died after a long and glorious reign and was succeeded by his son *Kunavira-singkai-ariyan*, a valiant monarch. He made war upon the king of *Kandi* for neglecting to pay the tribute and wrested from him a few districts, which he added to this kingdom and placed *Tamil* colonists in them.

This king rendered remarkable services to the *Nayakkar*, petty princes, who now ruled over *Mathurai*, having driven the *Pandiyan* away from it.

Like his father *Jeya-vira-singkai-ariyan*, he reigned long and died in peace.

He was succeeded by his son *Kanaka-suriya-singkai-ariyan* a weak prince. He ruled with neither justice nor firmness. Instigated and assisted by the *Vanniyar* his *Singhalese* subjects rose in arms against him and obliged him to quit the kingdom. He fled with his queen from *Nallur* under cover of night, leaving every thing behind and taking with him only his two sons who were both very young. The exiles reached *Vada-thesam* in safety, and, leaving the sons among the royal families of *Thiruk-kovalur* for the sake of their education, the king and queen set out on a pilgrimage to sacred places. They travelled far and visited many holy places, nor did they stop until they reached *Kashi*. From *Kashi* they retraced their steps and went to the *Kokarna Sivalayam*, where they stayed many years, observing religiously the annual *Siva-raththiri* feast. Their perseverance was at last rewarded. The king had a dream in which he and his wife were directed to go to *Mathurai* as a preliminary step towards the recovery of their throne. They concluded the long fast with due ceremonies and set out without a moment's delay. They first went to *Kovalur* where they were gladdened to see

Kanaka-suriya singkai-ariyan

His flight.

their sons grown in strength, beauty and martial bearing. The sons in their turn were gladdened at the sight of their parents as the lotus smiles at the embrace of the solar ray. But the joy of the parents knew no bounds when they discovered their sons' warlike preparations for recovering their patrimony. With hearts overflowing with gratitude the royal pilgrims thanked their generous friends and departed with their sons for *Mathürai*. The kingdom of *Mathurai* was then governed by a number of petty chiefs who had parcelled it out among themselves. Those chiefs assisted the fallen family with a good supply of men and means and enabled them to return to *Yalpanam*, which they did after having been seventeen years absent from it.

Vijayavaku. During the whole space of seventeen years the kingdom was in the hands of one *Vijaya-vaku*, a ringleader of the *Singhalese*, who had vaulted into the vacant throne as soon as he had learnt of the flight of the royal family. This usurper tyrannized over the *Tamils*, compelled them to adopt the *Singhalese* dress, manners and habits, and severely punished them if they followed their own ancient usages. The triumph of his tyranny was deemed so complete that he did not think it necessary to guard his capital with a strong army. Until he saw the enemy actually enter the capital by its western gate, the usurper fancied himself perfectly safe on his ill-gotten throne. To call out the soldiers of the city and form them into battle array was but the work of a moment. He took the command in person and displayed such daring feats of valour that the invaders were staggered for a moment, but *Para-rasa-sekaran*, the elder of the two princes, cut a passage with his sword through the opposing mass, approached *Vijaya-vaku*, sprang upon him like a lion, slew him with his own hand, and committed great havoc among his soldiers. The death of the leader was but the signal of defeat to the *Singhalese* soldiers, who fled in disorder and never attempted to take the field again.

Death of Vijaya-vaku.

The old monarch re-ascended the throne. His sons diligently searched for the adherents of the usurper and put them to the sword. Many *Singhalese* families left the kingdom in consequence of the rigour with which they were pursued, and withdrew to the *Kandiyan* territories, but those who remained behind quietly submitted to the *Tamils*.

Restoration of the old king.

The weight of old age began to press heavily on *Kanaka-suriya-singkai-ariyan* and he resigned his kingdom in favour of his eldest son *Para-rasa-sekeran*.

His abdication.

*Para-rasa-sekaran* was accordingly crowned king. One of his earliest acts was to change his name and that of his brother from *Para-rasa-sekara-singkai-ariyan* into *Singkaip-para-rasa-sekaran* and *Singkaich-cheka-rasa-sekaran*.

Para-rasa-sekaran.

*Para-rasa-sekaran's* queen and principal wife was *Irasa-lakkumi-ammal*, a daughter of the *Chola-rasan*. He took a

His wives.

second wife in the person of *Valli-ammai*, daughter of *Arasa-kesari* of the line of that famous *Malavan* of *Pon-patti-yur* in *Pandi*, who bore the distinguishing title of "The crown giver." Besides these two wives the king had a concubine of the name of *Mangkath-thammal* a woman from *Manakkudi*. By his queen he had two sons *Singka-vaku* and *Pandaram*; by *Valli-ammai*, *Para-nirupa-singkan* and three other children: and by *Mangkath-thammal* the concubine, one son, *Sangkili*. The king had the satisfaction of watching the growth of his children and their progress in literature and military science. But *Sangkili* early began to display that keen perception, indomitable courage and unscrupulous behaviour by which he was afterwards distinguished.

His children.

His brother.

The king's brother *Seka-rasa-sekaran* was an accomplished scholar. He encouraged learning, invited learned men from all parts of *Vadanadu* and *Thennadu* (northern and southern India) and introduced several valuable *Sanscrit* and *Tamil* books then not generally known in *Yalpanam*. Under his auspices a council of learning was established at *Yalpanam* and several new works were composed and published. *Yasakesari*, who was married to *Para Nirupa Singkan's* sister, translated the *Iraku-vamisam* from *Sanscrit* into *Tamil* poetry, a performance which was highly praised by the learned critics of the period who were assembled at *Thiruvalur* to hear it recited. *Seka-rasa-sekaran* himself wrote *Seka-rasa-*

Promotion of learning.

*sekaram*, an astrological work, and other books. He made frequent journeys to *Sethuk-karai* in order to consult learned men and ancient books from *Pandi-nadu* and other ancient places.

Supathidda-muni.

*Para-rasa-sekaran* was a just and vigorous sovereign. His reign was distinguished above all others by the arrival of a remarkable visitor to the court of *Yalpanam*. This was no less a personage than *Supathidda-muni* a son of *Siththa-muni* and grand son of *Akasthiya-muni* The king received him with all the marks of reverence due to his exalted sanctity and when he was seated, the king ventured to speak, saying " Lord and Master ! thou foretoldest future events to this thy slave's father. Thy slave has not been able to learn them properly. Deign to enlighten him with a knowledge of what shall happen to this kingdom." The *muni* replies " King ! your kingdom will flourish but a short time more. From a mistake of the auspicious moment at your coronation you will have no royal descendants to inherit your crown". To this the king says :—" Sir I have two sons by my queen, and many children by the other wife." The *muni* replies " True it is you have these children. But the first prince dies by poison and the second by the sword. Your second wife's eldest son will be deceived by smooth words into entrusting the government into the hands of *Sangkili*. *Sangkili* will tyrannize over your subjects and there will be disaffec-

His prophecy.

tion among them: and the kingdom will finally pass into the hands of strangers." The king continues "Lord! shall the kingdom ever return to my dynasty"? The *muni* replies, "It will first fall into the hands of the *Parangki*. He will destroy all the *Sivite* places of worship, spread the *Saththiya Vetham* with force of arms and rule forty years with an iron sceptre. The *Ulanthes* king will artfully overcome the *Parangki* and spread the *Ireppramathu Saththiya Vetham* with the power of the sword. He will prevent the people from worshipping their own gods and will make regulations abolishing the religious observances and ancient customs of the country. He will destroy all temples, build his own churches in various places, and compel all people to attend those churches. He will levy many taxes and otherwise oppress the people. His cruel reign will last more than one hundred and twenty years. The *Inthiresu* king will take the kingdom from the *Ulanthes* king and will proclaim to all persons liberty of conscience and freedom to build temples. He will reign 79 years with justice. And in the latter part of his reign the *Inthiresan* will not govern with justice as he will do at the commencement. When the time approaches that he shall lose the kingdom, preparations will be making to restore the sacred edifices built by *Singkai Ariya Maharasa* and by *Vijaya raja*. From motives of acquiring fame there will be many that will

The Portuguese.

The Dutch.

The English.

make the attempt to renew those edifices, but they will merely ruin themselves and find all their efforts prove ineffectual. Of those edifices only one, namely that which has been erected as protection for the northern ramparts of the city will be first completed by one favoured with the grace of *Siva*. Then will the others be begun and completed one after another. The restoration of the most important of the temples, *Kayilaya Nathar Koyil* and *Kayilaya Nayaki Amman Koyil* will be undertaken and accomplished by persons favoured by *Kayilaya Nathar*.

Restoration of temples.

When the *Inthiresu* man shall have reigned his allotted years the *Piragnchu rasa* and the *Ulanthes* king will wrest the kingdom from him by fraud and will reign from *Kolumpu*. Then will *Vala Singkan* make his appearance before them. To him they will deliver the government of the whole *Langka* and return to their own countries. After that *Puloka Singka Sakkira-varthi* son of *Ariya Singka Sakkiravarthi* will reign over the 57 countries from *Kanniya Kumari* to the *Imaya-malai*, under one umbrella. The sovereignty will never again come back to your descendants."

The French and the Dutch.

The *muni* departed. Notwithstanding his solemn assurance, his words did not make any strong impression on the king, for he was disposed partly to believe and partly to disbelieve what he had heard.

Death of the heir apparent.

Within a short time after this event the heir apparent met with his death suddenly. No body knew at the time that he died of poison administered by *Sangkili.* The king raised *Pandaram* the brother of the deceased to the dignity of Sub-king, and, leaving the care of the kingdom in his hands, went on a pilgrimage to *Kumpa-konam.* The king of the *Chola-thesam* also went to the same place for ablution, it being the *Maka Maka* festival. *Sangkili* who accompanied his father conducted himself with impropriety and was seized and thrown into prison by the *Cholan's* order. His father went to his rescue but was himself taken prisoner with a large part of his retinue. When *Para Nirupa Singkan* heard of the capture of his father he went with an armed force and offered battle to the *Cholan,* and though he was severely wounded in three places yet he continued the fight with the rage of a demon until he saw the enemy turn his back on him. The *Cholan* and his nobles fell into the victor's hands and were sent to prison to take the place of those of *Yalpanam* whom the *Cholan* had sent thither

The King's visit to Kumpakonam.

After three months the *Cholan* was released from prison and restored to his kingdom on his promise, accompanied with proper security, to pay tribute to *Para-rasasekaran. Para-nirupa-singkan's* wounds were now healed and the pilgrims returned to *Yalpanam.*

On reaching the capital the first act of the king was to shew his gratitude to *Para-nirupa-singkan.* He presented him with seven districts :—*Kalliyan kadu*, *Sandiruppai*, *Aruli*, *Achchuveli*, *Uduppiddi*, *Kachchay* and *Mallakam*, and perpetuated the gift by recording it on a plate of copper. He also appointed him next in rank to the Sub-king and shewed him other marks of distinction. These honors provoked *Sangkili's* envy, but he dissembled his feelings for the time. **Gift of land to Para-nirupa-singkan.**

*Para-nirupa-singkan* was an able physician, and he went to *Kandi* on the invitation of the king of that place to treat the *Kandiyan* queen for a painful colic that had baffled the skill of all other physicians of *Langka* and *Vada-thesam*. He effected the cure with a single dose of medicine and was able to depart from *Kandi* almost immediately after he had reached it. He left *Kandi* laden with the presents of a grateful court and reached home with great renown and an increased measure of popularity. **His skill as a Physician.**

*Sangkili* took advantage of the absence of *Para-nirupa-singkan* to plot for the kingdom. He lay in wait for the Sub-king *Pandaram* and slew him with his own hand, while that prince was taking a walk in his flower garden, unarmed and suspecting no danger. The murderer seized upon the throne and proceeded to exercise royal power. Appalled at the daring effrontery and fearing the fate of *Pandaram* the aged king relinquished his throne without an attempt to defend it. But not so *Para-nirupa-singkan* : he asserted his right to the **Sangkili usurps the throne.**

Wins over Para-nirupa-singkan.

throne in preference to his father's illegitimate offspring and was prepared to support his pretensions with the sword. The ambitious *Sangkili* at once saw the danger he was in. He went to *Para-nirupa-singkan* and gained him over with specious words. He represented that the kingdom was on the eve of a dreadful insurrection and that the *Vanniyar* were arming themselves for an invasion. The fear of an internal dissension in the royal family at what the credulous prince took to be a critical time induced him not only to allow *Sangkili* to retain the throne for the present and enjoy half the revenues of the kingdom, but even consented to become *Sangkili's* chief minister with the other half of the revenues. *Para-nirupa-singkan's* son, a youth named *Para-rasa-singkan* after his grand father, was placed in the government of the seven districts of his father.

This state of things did not last longer than *Sangkili* thought fit it should. Having attached the military to his cause by large donations, he ventured to interfere with his formidable minister. He first put a stop to the half, which *Para-nirupa-singkan* enjoyed, of the revenues, and assigned a limited sum as salary for the post of minister. He next removed *Para-rasa-singkan* from the government of the seven districts. The injured princes felt themselves too weak to take up arms in defence of their rights. But the old king resented *Sangkili's* treachery and wrote to the *Cholan* to discontinue the tribute which he paid annually to *Yalpanam* and the *Cholan* was only too glad to be thus relieved of what was both a burden and a disgrace to him.

For some time past the *Parangkis* frequented *Mannar* for purposes of trade. They first came to *Langka* in the year *Parithapi* corresponding with the *Saka* year 1428, in the reign of king *Parak-kirama-vaku* of *Kotta*, and having obtained his permission they commenced to trade in his territories, and by degrees extended their trade to this kingdom also. It was a sworn duty among the *Parangkis* to endeavour to spread their religion wherever they went. By the force of their preaching number of families embraced the *Saththiya vetham* at *Mannar*. As soon as *Sangkili* heard of this conversion he put six hundred persons to the sword without any distinction of age or sex. This took place in the month of *Adi* of the year *Kara*. His insane fury longed for more victims and he fell upon the *Buddhists*. The followers of *Buddhism* were all *Singhalese*, and of them there were many in this kingdom. By an order which he issued he expelled them beyond his limits and destroyed all their numerous places of worship. They betook themselves to the *Vannis* and the *Kandiyan* territories, and not one *Singhalese* remained behind nor ever after returned hither.

The Parangkis.

Their religion.

The massacre of their converts.

Expulsion of the Singhalese.

In the reign of *Vijaya Bahu* (the usurper) there was a numerous army of *Yavakar* in the king's pay. Their

The Malays.

The Malays. numbers underwent constant diminution by deadly feuds among themselves and by the oppression of kings. The remnants of them inhabited the villages of *Sava-kach-cheri* and *Savang-kodu* But *Sangkili* drove them also out of his kingdom.

Death of 49 Vanniyar. In this king's reign forty nine *Vanniyar* from *Then-nadu* set sail with the intention of joining their caste in the *Vannis.* The vessel which carried them was lost in the sea near *Nedun-thivu* and all were drowned. But their wives, the *Vannichchimar*, and one *Karaip-piddi-Vanniyan* and his wife, *Ammai-nachchiyar*, who sailed in other vessels, safely reached *Yalpanam* with their dependants and treasures and awaited here the arrival of their missing companions before proceeding to the *Vannis.* After a time the widowed *Vannichchimar* being reduced to poverty, they dispersed into various villages and subsisted upon the earnings of their slaves and dependants.

The Nambis. *Karaip-piddi-vanniyan* resided temporarily at *Kanthar-odai* then called *Odaikkurichchi.* He had sixty *Nambis* in his pay who served him as his swordsmen. Having violated the chastity of a daughter of one of these *Nambis*, he fell by the hand of the girl's enraged father who took him by surprize while he was engaged in prayer. His *Vannichchi* not knowing what to do with herself ran out into an open plain and there stabbed herself to death. The murder of the *Vanniyan* was avenged by the hand of the law, but his wealth was transferred to the royal treasury. The remaining *Nambis* went to *Sanarak-kuppam*, a neighbouring village, and, having no means of livelihood hired, themselves out to the *Sanar* and were trained by them in their hereditary occupation, namely, that of climbing the palmyra palm. From the circumstance of the *Nambis* having thus degraded themselves they came to be called *Naluvar*, from *naluvantrathu*, to fall off, now corrupted into *Nalavar*; and these *Nalavar* have ever since taken to climbing as their caste occupation. The Nambis. The Nalavar.

In this reign, the *Maravar* who had originally come from *Rama-natha-puram* and lived in *Maravan-pulavu* were proceeded against with rigour, and numbers of them were punished with death on account of the habitual thefts which they committed in the towns. The survivors fled from justice and found shelter in the jungles of *Pantiyan Thalvu*. The Maravar.

To compensate however for the large diminution of population which the tyranny of the king had caused, he received an accession of new subjects of various races who came from *Thenthesam* and settled in different parts of his kingdom, having been forced to leave their homes by a great famine which raged in both *Vada-thesam* and *Then-thesam*. New colonies.

A tumult having arisen among the inhabitants of *Vada-miradchi*, the king went in person to quell it. On

Sangkili hates Paranirupa-singkan.

his return his route lay through *Irupalai*, and when he arrived within its limits his musicians silenced their music. On inquiring the cause he was informed that he was within the territories which belonged to *Para-nirupa-singkan*, without whose permission the music could not be continued. *Sangkili* regarded this both as an insult to his dignity and an indication of the influence of *Para-nirupa-singkan* and desired much to deprive him of his territories and his influence, but found it unsafe to violate a grant publicly inscribed on copper. Hearing of an intended insurrection in favor of *Para-nirupa-singkan* and knowing that the sympathies of the *Vanniyar* and of the old king were with that prince, the artful *Sangkili* had again recourse to conciliatory measures. He allowed *Para-nirupa-singkan*, as at first to enjoy half the revenues of the kingdom and reinstated his son in the government of the seven districts. It was also from a motive of the same nature that *Sangkili* abstained from wearing a crown although he exercised all the powers of an independant sovereign. After a time when he felt he was again sufficiently strong to interfere with *Para-nirupa-singkan* he proposed to confer a title of honor upon him and his son. The title he proposed was that of *Muthaliyar*, one borne by the *Velalar* of *Then-tesam*. This was an artifice by which he hoped to turn away the attention of the people from his rivals' royal descent by reducing them to the rank of mere noblemen. The honor was declined with silent disdain, but the king caused it to be inscribed on the public register of titles. As this plan did not succeed as well as he expected, he next proposed to create *Para-nirupa-singkan* lord of 500 villages with the title of *Madap-pali*, a word composed of *madappam*, a cluster of 500 villages, and *ali*, a ruler. This too was declined like the former.

**The old king buries his wealth.**

The old king, who watched these events with apparent resignation, was long in hopes that the rightful heir would one day mount the throne. Seeing that nothing tended towards the accomplishment of that hope, but that *Sangkili* was daily becoming more and more powerful, he stealthily removed, by night, on the backs of elephants, his crown and sceptre with all his treasures and buried them in a dense forest belonging to the *Vannis*, at an inaccessible place where his predecessors had concealed theirs on former occasions ; and he placed the demon *Unmaththa Vayiravan* to keep watch over the place.

**Conspiracy against the King.**

The cruelty of *Sangkili* increased with his power. His subjects were not able to endure it any longer and all eyes were turned to *Para-nirupa-singkan*. This prince felt himself too weak to be able to wrest the kingdom from the usurper. But as he did not care who possessed his patrimony if he himself could not possess it, he thought of the *Parangkis*, whose feelings *Sangkili*

St. Francis Xavier.

had outraged by his massacre of their 600 converts in *Mannar.* The eloquent *Saveriyar* had since that massacre made several fruitless attempts to establish the faith again, but went away in disappointment. His calculating successors, however, who never abandoned the hope of being able some day to insinuate themselves and their religion into this kingdom, long cultivated a friendly but secret correspondence with *Para-nirupa-singkan,* as they knew that the state of feeling between the king and his minister was such that it would not be long before an opportunity would present itself to enable them to carry out their designs.

At this juncture of affairs the conduct of *Sangkili* brought about that opportunity, together with a train of events, which ultimately led to the ruin of himself and his kingdom. Having entertained an unlawful passion for the beautiful daughter of *Appa,* who was one of his ministers, *Sangkili* attempted to force the reluctant maid to submit to his wishes. *Appa* sought protection of *Para-nirupa-singkan,* which was readily granted. The girl was received into *Para-nirupa-singkan's* family and her father was despatched with a letter to *Kakkai-vanniyan,* a considerable personage, who had recently landed at *Urkavat-turai. Appa* returned with a reply from *Kakkai-vanniyan,* which he delivered to *Para-nirupa-singkan,* and, acting on the advice of the latter, went back to his usual business as if nothing had happened.

Outrage on Appa's daughter.

*Kakkai-vanniyan*, without a moment's delay, went to *Tharangkampadi* and assured the *Parangkis* that he would put *Yalpanam* into their hands. They hesitated at first, but persuaded by his oaths and entreaties, they fell in with his proposal and soon after landed at *Pannaith-thurai* disguised as traders. This took place in the month of *Vaikasi* of the year *Manmatha*. *Sangkili* was at first disposed to refuse them permission to land or trade, but being pointed out, by *Para-nirupa-singkan* and others, the great advantages of a foreign trade, he was persuaded to grant them a qualified permission, which gave them liberty to land during the day for purposes of trade, but which strictly enjoined that they should return to and remain in their vessels during night. When the fictitious trade had gone on for some time, the strangers were encouraged to approach the king, which they did with silks and other rare and valuable presents. The king received them graciously, and on hearing from them that they suffered extreme inconvenience as to their meals and other comforts of life, from having daily to go to and return from their vessels, he gave them permission to build a house on the sea shore for their wares, with liberty to remain in it during nights. This happened in the year *Supakiruthu* corresponding with the *Sakaptham* 1503. Pretending to act on this permission the *Parangkis* built a fort of earth and filled it with soldiers and weapons. The site which was selected for

The landing of the Portuguese disguised as traders.

They build a fort.

the fort was a secluded one: it was protected on the south by the sea and on the other three sides by a thick forest, so that no one saw it until one day the king went a hunting and came upon a fort and ramparts with a foreign flag waving over them. He could not at first believe his own eyes. His astonishment however was soon changed into rage when on blaming the *Parangkis* with having built the fort without his permission and on ordering them to pull it down, he was derisively told that they had his royal word for constructing a building and that if he now changed his mind they were not prepared to humour him.

The war. As might be expected a war ensued. The plain which lies on the west of the fort of *Nallur* opposite to the temple of *Viramakali-amman* was selected as the battle field On it were fought eleven battles in as many days. At first the fight was an ill-matched one. On one side there were the *Parangki* soldiers drawn up in battle array and armed with match-locks. But the soldier's duty was merely to point his matchlock at an enemy whom he was required to single out for the purpose, while it was the duty of an assistant to apply the fire to the priming of the musket. It frequently happened that no explosion followed the application of the fire. But whenever there was an explosion it was followed by deaths and wounds among the enemy. On the other side there were the *Tamils* with their swords and other weapons which were of no use to them until they came to close quarters with the enemy and if they once succeeded in coming to close quarters they became irresistible. At the eleventh day's fight the king and four hundred of his chosen warriors made such havoc upon the ranks of the *Parangkis* that the latter meditated a surrender. But the arrival of an unexpected reinforcement from *Tharangkampadi* raised their drooping spirits and enabled them to continue the war. Perceiving the disadvantage of their usual mode of warfare, the *Parangkis* made a change in it. They threw their onblesome muskets aside and fought like the *Tamils* with swords. But they still retained a number of musketeers whom they placed behind the shelter of a wood under cover of which they kept up a deadly fire. To counteract this, *Sangkili* placed trained men in proper places to send forth stones from slings, and other missiles upon the enemy. **Mode of fight.**

In these battles the king noticed the indifference shewn by *Para-nirupa-singkan* and the other ministers and expressed his displeasure at it, but they excused themselves by saying that their men were new to the *Parangki* mode of warfare. The king derided their pusillanimity, and taking with him a chosen band of heroes, he rushed into the thickest of the enemy and slew more than 1700 of them in the battle on the tenth day and 2400 on that of the eleventh.

The defeat of the Portuguese.

In the eleventh day's fight, the *Parangkis* lost their general and fled in confusion from the battle field. They were hotly pursued by *Sangkili* until they reached the forest, when pursuit became impossible. *Sangkili* entered their fort and slew every one he found there, sparing neither the sick and wounded nor the women and children. He removed all treasures he found in it to his own palace and razed the ramparts to the ground.

Sangkili's hasty act.

On returning to the city the soldiers celebrated their victory with a feast. In the midst of their revelry, some of them who were flushed with wine became violent and caused a slight disturbance. Their commander was at his evening prayers in the temple of *Viramakali-amman* and they would not obey the king's messengers. The king felt himself insulted and rushed out in person into their midst, but could not bring them to their senses. Blinded with rage, he ordered all the food prepared for the feast to be thrown into a deep pit, and covered over with earth. This was accordingly done and the hasty act disgusted the soldiers and completely estranged their affections from the king.

The *Parangkis* who fled from the battle field reached *Urkavat-turai* and were determined to sacrifice *Kakkai-vanniyan* to their fury. They believed that he had played them false and they told him that but for him they should not have suffered the loss, which they had, of 16000 of their men, in the war with *Sangkili*. Fortunately for *Kakkai-vanniyan* a messenger arrived just then with a letter from *Para-nirupa-singkan* addressed to *Kakkai-vanniyan*, expressing regret that the strangers had been defeated and that no open assistance had been given them by the natives. It also pointed out the necessity of joint action and invited the *Vanniyan* to join his forces to those of *Para-nirupa-singkan* and openly assist the strangers against the tyrant. Being assured, by the tenor of this letter, of the sincerity of the natives, the *Parangkis* determined to renew the fight on the morrow. The *Vanniyan* preceded them by night to *Nallur* and arranged with *Para-nirupa-singkan* the part which each should act. Very early in the morning a messenger despatched by *Para-nirupa-singkan* whispered into the ears of the commander of *Sangkili's* army that a spy was waiting for him without the walls of the city with some information of vital importance. The commander fell into the snare and followed the messenger through the eastern gate. He was introduced to the supposed spy whose artful eloquence so completely engrossed his attention that he forgot the army for the moment. In the meanwhile the *Parangkis* who were believed to have been vanquished besieged the western gate of the city. *Sangkili* heard the news with some surprise, but, with his usual intrepidity rushed to the scene with whatever

**The Portuguese take the field again.**

**Stratagem.**

**Besige the city.**

Kakkai-vanniyan's treachery.

men he could collect on the instant. He saw *Kakkai-vanniyan* already on the spot among his soldiers, and believing him to have come to his aid, he accosted him with these words "Friend! you have been slow hitherto but great is your kindness to-day in bringing me this timely aid." To testify his joy the king fell on the *Vanniyan's* neck and embraced him. The traitor pretended to return the compliment but held the king fast in his arms. The *Parangkis* rushed on the king as he stood struggling for liberty. The king's soldiers drew their swords, but *Para-nirupa-singkan* forbade them to use their weapons without the order of their commander. The king fell into the enemy's hands without a single sword being used in his defence, and his soldiers fled in dismay and disorder. *Sangkili* was thrown into prison and loaded with chains, and the commander of his army was soon after taken and put to death. Seeing that the white men were become masters of the kingdom, the old king, *Sangkili's* father, fled into the wilds of *Vanni*, carrying with him nothing but his trusty sword. The *Parangkis* having proclaimed a reward of 25,000 Rix-dollars for his apprehension, a greedy *Brahman*, formerly one of his ministers, went in search of him with a lime fruit and a tender cocoanut in hand. His search would have been fruitless had not the king, who espied him at a great distance, come forward to meet him, relying on the villain's sense of gratitude for favours which he had received from the king when he was his minister. After the usual salutations and enquiries on both sides, the *Brahman* presented the cocoanut to the king, cut it open with the king's sword, which the king handed to him for the purpose, and squeezed the juice of the lime into it. As the king bent forward to drink the water from the cocoanut, the other severed his head from the body by a single stroke with the king's own sword and brought the head to the *Parangkis* in great exultation. The *Parangkis*, horrified at the bloody act, assured the ungrateful minister that although they had set no price on the king's head but had only proclaimed a reward for the king's apprehension, yet he, the minister, should undoubtedly have the price of his act; and accordingly they caused him to be executed on the very spot on which he stood.

Death of the old king.

The *Parangkis* next brought *Sangkili* to trial. *Sangkili* was placed before the seat of justice and charged first with having exercised regal powers without having been duly crowned: secondly, with having usurped the throne from his father: thirdly, with having murdered the princes of the realm: and fourthly, with having oppressed the people and massacred many of them. He was convicted of all the charges and sentenced to be decapitated. The sentence was immediately carried into effect at the threshold of the nearest temple. On hearing this, *Sangkili's* wife committed suicide, and his children the *Parangkis* sent away to *Tharangkam-padi*.

Death of Sangkili.

Reward to the traitors.

*Kakkai-vanniyan* received all the marks of honor due to his services and retired to *Urkavat-turai.*

In reward for the services of *Para-nirupa-singkan*, the *Parangkis* added the two districts of *Nallur* and *Mathakal* to the seven that he owned before. They confirmed him in his post of chief minister, presented him with a large sum of money, appointed his son governor over his nine districts and distinguished him and his family with special marks of favour and respect. Having by these means, succeeded in establishing their rule firmly on the land, the *Parangkis* now began to interfere in matters of religion. They broke down all the *Sivalayams* and spread the *Saththiya-vetham*, but out of respect to *Para-nirupa-singkan* they spared the temple of *Nallur* and those in the neighbourhood of *Kirimalai* and allowed public worship to be continued in them as before.

Parangkis destroy the fort of Nallur.

Thus the reign of the *Parangkis* commenced in the month of *Ani* of the *Sakaptha* year *Kalavuththi*. The *Parangkis* took up their residence at *Nallur*, but they pulled down its walls and fortifications and with the materials, built a new fort, several offices and dwelling houses for their officers. They cleared the neighbourhood of the forest and made it habitable for man.

*Para-nirupa-singkan* died in the 9th year of the *Parangki* rule. Not only did the *Parangkis* allow his corpse the rights of cremation, but they secured to it the performance of all the customary ceremonies and decreed a public mourning in honor of his memory. They afterwards raised his son to the office of counsellor but applied to him the titles of *Muthali* and *Madappali* as they found them entered in the public registry of *Sangkili's* reign.

Para-rasa Singkan's death.

Like his father, *Para-rasa-singkan* enjoyed the favour and confidence of the *Parangkis*, and was highly respected by the people. When his death approached he sent for his children, seven sons and one daughter, and distributed his districts among them. Hegave *Nallur* and *Kalliyan-kadu* to *Alakanmai-valla-muthali* and placed him in his palace of *Nallur*. He gave *Mallakam* to *Thanapala-singka-muthali*: *Sandiruppai* to *Vetti-vela-yutha-muthali*: *Arali* to *Visaya-theyventhira-muthali*: *Ach-chuveli* to *Thida-vira-singka-muthali*: *Uduppiddi* to *San-thira-sekara-mappano-muthali*: *Kachchai* to *Iraya-redna-muthali*: and *Mathakal* to his daughter *Vetha-valliyar* whom he bestowed in marriage on a *Velalan* of that district.

Persecution against Saivites.

When *Pararasa-singkan* was dead, the *Parangkis* began to destroy all the remaining temples. A pious *Brahman* of the name of *Parasu-pani-ayyar* anticipated the emissaries of the *Parangkis* and threw all the images and furniture of the *Kiri-malai* temples into a deep well for safety and covered them over with earth. *Sangkili*, a *Pandaram* employed as a servant in *Kantha-*

*suvami* temple, ran away to *Batticaloa*, carrying with him the copper inscription relating to the origin and formation of the temples of *Nallur* and the rules and directions for their management. The descendants of the *Brahman Kangkatharar* quitted *Nallur* and went to live in *Nirveli* and *Vadamiradchi*.

Mathakkar appointed.

The office of Prime minister or chief counsellor was abolished and four *Mathakkar* were appointed instead. *Iraya-redna-muthali's* son *Sola-singkach-chenathi-rasa-muthali* for the east : *Visaya Theyventhira-muthali* for the west : *Alakanmai-valla-muthali's* son *Rasa-vallapa-muthali* for the south : and *Thida-vira-singka-muthali's* son *Kumara-suriya-muthali* for the north.

About this time a number of families came from *Karaikkal* and other places, and settled in *Vadduk-koddai* (Batticotta) and *Kara-thivu* and other Islands.

The *Parangkis* commenced to visit Ceylon in the reign of King *Parakkirama vaku* of *Kotta*, who in the *Saka* year 1428, gave them permission to trade with his subjects. The *Parangkis* carried on their trade not only within that king's districts, but in those of this kingdom also. They had an establishment at *Mannar* where by means of their preaching, they converted to the *Saththiya-Vetham* numbers of families, of whom king *Sangkili* massacred six hundred in the year *Kara*. At the news of this massacre, *Savariyar* (Xavier) a powerful preacher from *Puruththikal-thesam* made strenuous but fruitless efforts to establish the *Saththiya-Vetham* again in *Mannar*. After him, his successors continued the efforts until the year *Manmatha*, when they succeeded, as related above, in first getting themselves introduced to *Sangkili* in the character of traders, through the intercession of *Para-nirupa-singkan*, and afterwards, in *Supa-kiruthu-varudam*, corresponding with the *Sakaptha* year 1503, in building a fort of sand in *Yalpanam*.

In the meantime, the *Ulanthesar*, who first arrived at *Kandi* in the month of *Thai* of the year *Iraththadchi*, gained the friendship of the king of that place, *Vimala-tharuma-maha-rasa*, by their promise to support him against the *Parangkis*, with whom he was then at war. The cause of the war was as follows :—A former king of *Kandi*, who had been driven out of his kingdom, had delivered his daughter, an infant, to the *Parangkis* for safety. They removed her to *Mannar*, educated her in their own faith, gave her the name of *Thona-Kaththarina* (Dona Catharina), and now assumed the field against *Vimala-tharuma-maha-rasa*, in order to set her up on the throne of her ancestors. But with the aid of the *Ulanthesar*, the king defeated the *Parangkis*, captured the princess and made her his wife. In the year *Adchaya*, the good understanding between the *Kandiyan* king and the *Ulanthesar* was brought to a violent termination. In a fit of intoxication, the admiral of the *Ulanthes* fleet insulted *Vimala-tharuma-rasan* and expi-

The Dutch.

ated the offence with his own life and the lives of all his attendants who were on shore with him at the time. This made the *Ulanthesar* withdraw to *Kolumpu*, where they built a fort in its neighbourhood. But the *Parangkis* interrupted their designs and compelled them to go further northwards.

The Danes. In the meanwhile, a new nation made its appearance in *Langka*, the *Thenmarkar* (Danes). They made the usual offers of disinterested assistance to the king of *Kandi*, as the *Parangkis* and the *Ulanthesar* had done before them. Taught by bitter experience, the wary king refused to enter into negotiations with the new adventurers; and they betook themselves to their ships and returned to their country without effecting anything. This event took place in the year *Vilampi*, i.e., three years before the *Parangkis* commenced the fort of *Yalpanam*, and four and nine years before they finished the forts of *Trincomalie* and *Batticaloa* respectively.

In the year *Parpava*, the *Parangkis* completed the stone fort of *Yalpanam*. But in the following year they lost the forts of *Trincomlie*, *Batticaloa* and *Negombo* to the *Ulanthes*, from whom, however, they recovered *Negombo* back in a very short time.

On the thirtieth day of *Karththikai*, in the *Saka* year *Kshaya*, the *Ulanthesar* captured *Anthony Amral*, the *Parangki* Governor of *Yalpanam*, on his way to *Kolumpu* from *Mannar*, and cast him into prison. They followed up this advantage by attacking the fort of *Mannar*, which they took on the 9th day of the month of *Masi* in the year *Kalavuththi*. Thence they proceeded to *Yalpanam* in the beginning of the month of *Pangkuni* of the same year, and having placed their soldiers in all directions around the Peninsula, cut off all communications from without. But the fort of *Yalpanam* remained in the hands of the *Parangkis*, and the *Ulanthesar* saw no immediate prospect of taking it. About the end of that month, one *Ulaku-kavala Muthali* of *Karathivu* came to their aid. He was a considerable *Velalan* of *Chola-nadu*, and, having been implicated in his own country in treasonable transactions against his king, he had been obliged to save his life by flight. He founded a settlement which he named *Kala-pumi* in the Island of *Karathivu* and lived among his dependants in great wealth and splendour. He luxuriously entertained the *Ulanthesar* when they landed in that island and promised to lead them to certain victory, if they would but wait patiently for a fitting opportunity. They waited, but over three months elapsed before an opportunity presented itself. The *Parangkis* had a custom not to sleep during nights in troublous times, so that they might be ready at all moments to repulse a night attack. And to enable them the more easily to keep awake, they amused themselves with dancing and singing. One night while they were so occupied, *Ulaku-kavala-muthali*

Mannar taken.

introduced the *Ulanthesar* into the fort, by means of a trap-door which he had caused to be kept open for the purpose. The next morning, people were amazed to find the *Ulanthesar* celebrating a feast of joy, and their flag waving over the ramparts, while *Parangki* corpses lay choaking the moats around. This happened on the 9th day of the month of *Ani* of the year *Vilampi*, corresponding with the year 1571 of the *Salivakana-sakaptham*.

Introduction of the Reformation.

The first public act of the *Ulanthesar* was to introduce the *Irappiramathu-Saththiya-vetham*. In respect of the Civil Government, they appointed *Puthaththampi*, a *Velalan*, to be *Muthali* for the revenue branch of the government, and *Manuel Anthirasu* a man of the *Kuru-kula* caste, to be *Muthali* for the writing branch. An intimacy sprung up between the two *Muthalimar*, and *Anthirasu*, being one day at *Puthaththmpi's* house on an invitation to dinner, happened to have a sight of his host's wife, a woman of transcendent beauty, and was inflamed with a violent passion for her. She was a sister of *Kayilasa Vanniyan* and had inherited the haughty spirit and stern morality, by which her ancestors were distinguished among the nobility. She received *Anthirasu's* wicked proposal with indignation and displayed her resentment by subjecting his messenger to the ignominious punishment of being lashed with a broom. The spurned suitor meditated revenge and planned a diabolical one. He procured *Puthaththampi's* signature to a sheet of blank paper, pretending that it was to be filled up with an order for the removal of government timber from *Kachchaiththurai.* But the paper was actually filled up with treasonable matters, couched in the form of a letter from *Puthaththampi* to the *Parangkis,* offering to assist them to recover the kingdom if they would but make the attempt. A messenger, who was found carrying the letter, was seized and brought before the Governor. And witnesses were not wanting to fill up the details of the wicked farce. However, a strict investigation having been instituted, *Puthaththampi's* innocence was completely established. But the Governor of *Yalpanam,* who was a friend of *Anthirasu,* allowed himself to be influenced by *Anthirasu's* arguments and entreaties, and *Puthaththampi* was sentenced to death. The sentence was executed in a great hurry, before news could reach the governor's brother, *Puthaththampi's* most powerful and intimate friend, who was then absent at *Urkavat-turai,* building the *Kadat-koddai* there. On the representation of *Kayilaya-Vanniyan,* who went to *Kolumpu* for the purpose, the governor of *Yalpanam* and his friend, *Anthirasu,* were, in the month of *Puraddasi,* in the year *Vilampi,* ordered to proceed to *Kolumpu.* On their way thither, the former suffered ship-wreck and was drowned, the latter was crushed to death by a wild elephant.

Puthaththampi and Andirado.

In the same year there was a heavy inundation at *Urkavat-turai*, by which a large number of men and beasts lost their lives.

The *Ulanthesar* rewarded *Ulakukavala Muthali* with immense riches, made him *Muthali of the gate*, and used their friendly offices in procuring a marriage between him and the sister of *Marapa-luyarntha-muthali*. They confirmed *Marapa-luyarntha-muthali* in his office of head of the treasury, which he had held under the former Government.

On the death of *Ulakukavala-muthali*, his office and dignities were conferred on his son *Raya-thungka-muthali*. This *Muthali* married his cousin, one of the seven daughters of *Marapal-uyarntha-muthali*, and the nuptials were celebrated under the auspices of the Governor and his chief officers. When *Marapal-uyarntha-muthali* died, one of his sons-in-law, *Puloka-muthali*, was raised to the president-ship of the treasury and the dignities attached to that office.

The Moors. During the supremacy of the *Ulanthesar*, a colony of *Sonakar* came from *Kayilpaddanam* and other places and settled in *South-mirisuvil*, the name of which they changed into *Usan*. They were originally *Tamils* by race but had embraced the *Mukammathu-matkam* by the compulsion or persuasion of one *Santhach-chaivu*. Their chief means of subsistence was trade, which they carried on from fair to fair in *Savukach-cheri*, *Kodi-*

*kamam*, *Eluthu-madduval*, and *Mukavil*. After a time they abandoned *Usan* and founded a new settlement in *Nallur*, on and around the site of *Kantha-Suvami-Koyil*. The *Tamils* viewed their presence with displeasure, as they thought that it might be detrimental to the cause of their religion when the time should come for the restoration of the temple. They tempted the *Sonakar* to leave the place, with money and entreaties, which when they found unavailing, they had recourse to a plan that proved effectual. They put a quantity of pig's flesh into the wells of their enemy by night. When the defilement was discovered, the *Sonakar* were in great distress of mind. They could neither drink the water nor cook their meals with it, and they saw themselves driven to the necessity of choosing between starvation on one hand and emigration on the other. They chose the latter and sold the place for whatever money they could get from the *Tamils* and retired to the east of *Navanthurai*. Before they left, they, however, had made a compact by which they retained to themselves the right of visiting the spot, at stated times, for purposes of *Muhammathan* worship even when a *Tamil* temple should happen to be afterwards built upon it.

A great commotion having arisen in Southern India about this time, various races of its inhabitants left their homes and sought peace and comfort in foreign countries. Many *pira-mana* families, both of the *Vishnu* and *Saiva Samayams*, came from *Uththara-kosa-mangkai* and settled in *Kara-thivu*. Also many *Pallar* left their homes in *Chola-nadu*, in the hope of finding employment in the fields belonging to the *Velalar* in *Yalpanam*. They came in such large numbers that most of them met with disappointment. Some returned to *Chola-nadu*, but others remained behind and took to climbing the palmyra palm. The *Sanar*, whose occupation climbing legitimately was, and who had lost much of their living when the *Nambis* (*Nalavar*) took to it, were now almost completely deprived of it, and they took to new occupations. They either hired themselves as domestic servants to the whiteman or found profitable employment in making oil and in fishing with the net. The *Nalavar* and the *Pallar* now felt in their turn that they too were too numerous for the newly acquired industry, notwithstanding that they had elbowed the *Sanar* out of it; and many of them were obliged to sell themselves as slaves to the *Velalar* and other high castes.

The Pallar.

Besides the *Pallar* and the *Nalavar*, there was another and a better caste of slaves in the country known as the *Koviyar*, a corruption of the word *Koyilar* i. e. " slaves of the *Koyils*," for, these people had originally been servants of temples, but afterwards had, through poverty, sold themselves as slaves to temples. When the temples were destroyed by the *Parangkis*, the temple managers

The Koviyar.

sold the *Koviyar* to private purchasers as they had no occasion for their services.

Some time after this, a number of poor but good caste people were brought from *Vadathesam* and sold here for slaves, and they have acquired the name *Vadasiraik Koviyam.*

As the slave-trade has increased gradually, the Government have taken it into their own hands, in order to increase their revenue.

The Dutch policy.

The increase of revenue and the spread of religion are the chief concerns of the *Ulanthesar*. Not merely have they increased the old rates of taxation and laid several new taxes but they have also invented new sources of revenue. They sell patents of nobility and have put a high price upon the privilege of being served by the *Pokis, Koviyar* and other dependant castes.

The *Pokis* are a race of palanquin bearers who were brought out from *Vadatnesam* for the exclusive service of the *Tamil* kings and distinguished by the name of *periya-siviyar.*

The *Ulanthesar* have, by force of their authority, stopped the observance of all other religions than the [illegible]-*pramathu Saththiya-Vetham.* They have divided [illegible]*nam* into thirty two parishes, in each of which they have built a church, and placed a minister in each church. They have published a proclamation requiring every one to attend their churches for worship, instruction and

The Dutch policy

marriage, and to observe all the other rites and ceremonies of their religion. It is their avowed intention that there should be no other religion in this country than theirs. Such is the policy of their government—a policy which they are carrying out with extreme vigour.

THE END

# APPENDIX.

TO THE

# YALPANA-VAIPAVA-MALAI.

# APPENDIX I.

## IRADCHATHAR.

The Iradchathar are a race of Titans. Their origin and history are given in the Tamil Iramayanam thus:—

When Piraman created all living things, he created the wicked Iradchathar also. Of these there were two brothers Ethi and Pirakethi. The latter begat Viththukkesan. Viththukkesan had a wife who was attached to him as the soul to the body and as the andil bird to its mate, and she accordingly followed him wherever he went. In the course of her wanderings she gave birth to a son whom she abandoned on the spot in order to follow her husband as was her wont. Sivan took the helpless infant under his protection and gave him immortality. The infant grew up, married a Kantharuva virgin and begat Maliyavan, Sumali, and Mali. These three brothers went to the Maha-Meru mountains, performed austerities and became invincible.

In a former age of the world in a trial of strength between Varunan (the wind) and the snake Vasuki, the snake spread his hood and shut out wind from the universe. Varunan beat on the outspread hood with all his might but could not displace it. The gods and all animated creation were in immediate danger of their lives, having no air to breathe. Vasuki took pity on them and, slightly lowering his head, allowed a small passage to his adversary who thereupon rushed in with such force that he carried away three of the 1,000 peaks of the golden mountain (Maha-meru,) and cast one of them into the ocean.

Where the peak fell, there the architect of the gods chose his site to build a city for Maliyavan, Sumali and Mali, and he built one worthy to be called by the gods Ilangkai, from its inaccessible situation. Here the brothers lived with their wives; and their children grew up like "Death, Fire, Poison, the anger of the wicked, the wealth of the unlearned, and the sin of the king who exacts a tax of more than a sixth part from his subjects." The gods and sages unable to endure the oppression of the Iradchathar went in a body with their complaints to the Court of Sivan. Sivan directed them to Vishnu, destroyed the forces of the Iradchathar and drove them to the infernal regions.

Pulasthiya-muni, a son of Piraman, sat in religious meditations on the Maha-meru mountains, but was daily disturbed by the songs and sports of a troop of virgins who went thither to gather flowers. His patience being at length exhausted he pronounced the curse that they should become mothers if they approached him again. One of them who did not hear the curse approached him unwittingly, By the effect of the curse she became pregnant, and in due time brought forth a son, Vaichchirava. Vaichchirava begat Vaichchiravanan or Kuveran. The latter denied himself all food, rest and sleep in the performance of austerities. In reward for them he was appointed guardian of wealth and regent of the North, and was also presented with a magic chariot that moved in the air, was swifter than the swiftness of the mind and capable of containing the inhabitants of the universe. He went and occupied Ilangkai-ma-nakaram, from which Vishnu had compelled his forefathers to retire. But Sumali could not bear to see his own kingdom in the hands of a stranger. He devised that at least one of his progeny should have it, and bade his daughter go to Vaichchirava the father of Kuveran. Vaichchirava joined her, and she gave birth to three sons and one daughter. Iravanan, the eldest, a son, was born with ten heads and twenty hands. Her second child, also a son, Kumpakannan, had a pair of tusks like the elephant. The third was a daughter, Surpanakai, who had a voice like that of thunder. The last was Vidanan or Vipishanan, a pious sage. Kumpakannan habitually lived on human flesh. Surpanakai made meal of every man that refused to satisfy her lust. Iravanan and Kumpakannan performed austerities for ten thousand years each, Vidanan for five thousand years. At last Piraman appeared to them and promised to grant them whatever they might ask. Vidanan said "grant that I may not swerve from the path of rectitude even in times of the greatest affliction." Iravanan enumerated a variety of entities and prayed that he might not suffer death from any of them. But as he despised the human race he omitted "man" in his enumeration. Kumpakannan was prepared to ask for many and extraordinary gifts, but at the instigation of the gods, Sarasvathi (the goddess of learning) sat on his lips and made him utter the word "sleep." The god granted them each his request as it came from his lips.

Now all the Iradchathar returned to the earth from the infernal regions whither they had been driven by Vishnu, and having made Iravanan their king, they meditated an attack on Lanka-nakari their ancient capital. Kuveran evacuated it as soon as he perceived their design and transferred his wealth to Alakai on the Imaiya mountains. And Iravanan took possession of the vacant city.

The above account has been condensed from the first and second Padalams of the seventeenth book of Iramayanam entitled the "Uththirakandam". To complete the narrative it remains only to add that this Iravanan carried away Sitha, the wife of Iraman, the son of king Thasarathan of Mithilai, and imprisoned her in Ceylon. The bereaved husband made war upon the ravisher, slew him in single combat and gave his kingdom to Vidanan (the brother of Iravanan) who had deserted Iravanan and joined the conqueror at the very inception of the war (Vira cheritra and Mahanataka of Wilson).

The Singhalese annals fix the date of Ravana's death at 2387 B. C. whilst Sir W. Jones informs us that Rama about 1810 B. C. conquered Silan, a few centuries after the flood,

In the Mahaparatham the events of which are laid in the third uga of the world, we find an emissary of the Pandavar proceeding to Ceylon and receiving the submission of the Vidanan mentioned in the Iramayanam. On that occasion Vidanan is said to have sent to the Pandavar among other gifts a present of 14 palmyra palms of the size of nature, made of solid gold. See Book II entitled the Sapaparuvam Chapter I entitled the Irasasuyachcharukkam.

The Mahaparatham gives a detailed account of Piraman's creation to which the Iramayanam but merely alludes.

" Piraman is the author of creation. He had several children who sprang from the various parts of his body. Of these Thakkan, a son sprang from the big toe of his right foot, and Tharani, his only daughter, from the big toe of his left foot.

Thakkan joined Tharani and begat fifty daughters, of whom he bestowed ten on the Manu called Tharuman (a son of Piraman) twenty-seven on Chanthiran (the moon, a male diety) and the remaining thirteen on Kasipan (a grandson of Piraman.)

Kasipan's progeny are Iraniyan, Pirakalathan, Palichchakkiravarththi, Pana Suran, and other Asurar, an innumerable host : Iruku: the sixteen Kantharuvar : the Apsara girls : the celestial cows : the Siththar : the Kites : and the Nakars.

The other descendants of Piraman are Pirahaspathi (i, e. planet Jupiter) who is the Kuru of the gods : the rishis : Vichchiravaku, an Arakkan : the K narar : the Kimpirudar : the Vasukkal : the Kanthiruvar: Visvakarma (the celestial Architect) : the Uriththirar : the Asvenithevathaikal : Sukkiran (the planet Venus, a male diety, the teacher of the Asurar.) Also crows, doves, kites, owls, alcedos, pigs, monkeys, elephants, lions, tigers, deer, trees creepers, herbs, grass, horses, and other animals, plants and things having life (Book I. Athiparuvam, Chapter II. Pirapanchar-utpavach-charukkak-kathai.)

The *Tamils* reckon 18 classes of rational beings. They are,

1. Asurar, children of *Diti* by *Kasyapa* are, demons of the first order and in perpetual hostility with the gods.

From *a* neg. and *Sura* a deity

2. Amarar-immortals, i. e. souls enjoying bliss in Siverga the heaven of Indra.

From *a* neg. and *mara* what dies

3. Siththar—men who have become like gods in this world while yet retaining the human body.

From *Sidha* to be perfect.

4. Thaiththiyar—demons, Asurar, Titans or giants.

From *Diti*, their mother.

5. Kerudar—the plural of Kerudan, a being between a man and a bird (the kite) and sovereign of the feathered race. He is the son of Kasiyappa by Vinathai.

From *garuth* a wing. and *tti* to fly.

6. Kinnarar—demi-gods attached to the service of Kuvera, celestial musicians having the head of a horse with the human figure.

From *nara* a man, with *kin* what? (asked in contempt.)

7. Niruthar—demons, fiends.

From *Nairirtha* a proper name for the ruler of the South-west quarter.

8. Kimpurudar—demi-gods, celestial musicians, people inhabiting the region above the clouds, near the Himalacuta.

From *purusha* man. See Kinnarar.

9. Kantharuvar—celestial musicians.

From *Gandherba*, name of a place.

10. Iyakkar—yaksha—demigods, attendants especially on Kuveran and employed in the care of his gardens and treasures. Kuveran was himself a yaksha and bore the title of "Friend of Sivan"

From *yaksha* to worship.

11. Vigngnaiyar—celestial musicians, sages.

From *vignanam* music, learning.

12. Puthar—Bhuta—demigods, ghosts, goblins, malignant spirits haunting cemetries, lurking in trees, animating carcases, deluding or devouring human beings, they are attendants of Sivan, Ganesha &c.

From *bhu* to exist.

13. Pisasar—Pishasa—a sprite, a fiend, a malevolent being between an infernal imp and a ghost, but always fierce and malignant.

From *pishitha* flesh, and *asha* to eat.

14. Antharar—ærial beings.

From *anthara,* space.

15. Munivar—Sages who have attained divine nature.

From *man* to be revered.

16. Urakar—Snakes.

From *uras* the breast and *gam* to go.

17. Akayavasikal—inhabitants of the air

From *Akas* the air.

18. Pokapumiyar—Souls which enjoy bliss in the heavens of the particular deities whom they worshipped in this world. For dieties have each his own heaven.

Of these eighteen classes the Asurar, Thaiththiyar, Niruthar, Iyakkar and Puthar seem to partake of the nature of one another.

The Asurar are also known by the following names.

1. Thakuvar—a Tamil word—masters, because they once ruled over gods and men.
2. Thanusar—children of *Danu,* daughter of *Daksha,* wife of *Kasiyappa.*
3. Thaiththiyar—*Ditis'* children.
4. Nisasarar—night walkers.

The Iyakkar are also known by the following names.

1. Iradchathar—Tamil form of Rakshasa from the root *raksha* to preserve (Kuveran's wealth.)
2. Arakkar—same as the above.
3. Irakkathar—same as the above.
4. Idumpar—haughty persons.
5. Salakadangkadar—those who haunt cemetries.
6. Pisithasanar—flesh eaters.
7. Yathuthanavar—children of *Danu.*

In addition to the above eighteen classes there are the *Milechchar* or foreigners some of whom are scarcely allowed to be human beings. The *Milechchar* originally known to the sanscrit people are

1. Paundrakas—inhabiting beyond Bengal and Behar and south of the Ganges,
2. Odras—Uriyas.
3. Dravidas—inhabiting Southern India.
4. Cambojas—Arachosians.
5. Yavanas—Greeks or Baktrians.
6. Sakas—inhabiting Sacha regio.
7. Paranas—Paropamisans.
8. Pahlavas—Persians.
9. Chinas—Chinese.
10. Kiratas—Generally mountaineers, specially of the Imayas.
11 Deradas—Daradæ.
12. Khasas—Schuti.

The term Kirata is worthy of remark. Its Tamil forms are Kirathan (sing) and Kirathar (pl.) and has the following terms for its synonymes.

Aviyar—life-men, agriculturists.

Kanavar—foresters.

Vedar—huntsmen, identical with the Singhalese Veddhas.

Kuravar—gypsies.

Kuliyar—dwarfish imps, barbarians, hunters, attendants on Sivan.

Kolaignar—murderers, killers.

Savarar—carcass-eaters.

Pullar—people of low value.

Maravar—warriors.

Murudar—musicians.

From a comparison of the various existences enumerated above and the names and acts ascribed to each there can be no doubt as to there being a close connection, if not an actual identity between the Rakshasas of the Vaipavamalai and the Yakkhos of the Singhalese, notwithstanding that in the Sarvajnalankari an enumeration of sentient beings is given thus; Gods, Brahmas, Asuras, Men, Nagos, Supannas, Yakshas, Rakshas, Siddhas, Widdhyadharas and others. The notion which the Singhalese attached to their term Yakkhos may be gathered from the subjoined extracts from their books shewing the moral and physical qualities which the Yakkhos possessed, compared with those of the gods, men, nakar and other rational existences. The Yakkhos of the native historians were once the owners and rulers of Ceylon as the etymology of their name indicates and history and tradition prove. In the time of Buddho the Yakkhas inhabited Langka. They had a garden of assembly at Bintenne for their chiefs and, when they were there in such large numbers as to cover a space of 12 square leagues, Buddho appeared in their midst, produced miraculous rains, tempests and darkness, and so terrified them that they conferred the whole Island on him and betook themselves to the isle of Giri (Rajaratnacari. p.p. 16-18.) Some think that this isle of Giri was situate near Mannar but others hold that its site is occupied by the two Basses. (Rajavali p. 170.) When the yakkhos were gone, the devos to the number of 100,000 came and served Buddho with their chief, Saman, a tutelary deity of Saffragam, usually confounded with Lakshaman the brother of Rama. (Rajaratnacari p. 18.) Some of these devos had been human beings in their former existences. They served not Buddha only but even Asoko in a later period, to whom they procured valuable towels.

Buddha was not altogether successful in driving away the yakkhos from Langka, for 700 of them concealed themselves with their families in the wilderness of Tammanawannia and thus escaped banishment. They afterwards came out and dwelt in the villages Layale and Laggale. (Rajavali p. 172.)

"The ruler of the world, the great sage, in the midst of a great assembly of devatas, addressed this celebrated injunction to Sakko, who stood near him. One Wijayo, the son of Sihabahu, king of the land of Lala, together with seven hundred giants, officers of state, has landed on Langka. Lord of devos! my religion will be established in Langka. On that account thoroughly protect, together with his retinue, him and Langka."

The devoted king of devos having heard these injunctions of the successor (of former Buddhos) assigned the protection of Langka to the devo Uppulwanno (Vishnu.) He, in conformity to the command of Sakko, instantly repaired to Langka and in the character of a paribajako (devotee) took his station at the foot of a tree.

With Wijayo at their head, the whole party approaching him, inquired; "Pray, devotee, what land is this?" He replied, "The Land Lanka." Having thus spoken he blessed them by sprinkling water on them out of his jug; and having tied (charmed) threads on their arms, departed through the air.

A menial yakkhini (named Kali) assuming a canine form presented herself. One (of the retinue) though interdicted by the prince, followed her, saying, "In an inhabited village (alone) are there dogs."

There (near a tank) her mistress, a yakkhini, was seated like a devotee at the foot of a tree spinning thread which appeared like shining gold. The name of this "female demon or goddess" was Kuveni. She had been born with three breasts, in respect of which there was a prophecy that one of them would vanish at the approach of him who was destined to be her husband. The odd breast having now disappeared, she awaited for the speedy fulfilment of the prophesy. (Rajavali pp. 172, 173.)

Seeing this tank and the devotee seated near it he bathed and drank there; and while he was taking some (edible) roots and water from that tank, she started up and thus addressed him, "Stop thou art my prey." The man, as if he was spell bound, stood without the power of moving. By the virtue of the charmed thread she was not able to devour him; and though intreated by him the yakkhini cast him bellowing into a subterraneous abode. In like manner, the seven hundred flowers also she one by one lodged in the same place.

All these persons not returning, Wijayo becoming alarmed, equipping himself with the five weapons of war, proceeded after them; and examining the delightful pond he could perceive footsteps leading down only into the tank; and he there saw the devotee. It occurred to him. "My retinue must surely have been seized by her." "Pray, why dost thou not produce my ministers?" said he. "Prince," she replied, "from ministers what pleasures canst thou derive? Do drink and bathe (ere) thou departest." Saying to himself, "Even my lineage this yakkhini is acquainted with", rapidly proclaiming his title and bending his bow he rushed at her. Securing the yakkhini by the throat with a "narachana" ring, with his left hand seizing her by the hair, and raising his sword with his right hand, he exclaimed "Slave, restore me my followers (or) I will put thee to death." The yakkhini terrified, implored that her life might be spared. "Lord! spare my life, on thee I will confer this sovereignty: unto thee I will render the favours of my sex and every other service according to thy desire." In order that he might not be involved in a similar difficulty again he made the yakkhini take an oath. (Thereafter) while he was in the act of saying, "Instantly produce my followers," she brought them forth. Declaring "These men must be famished," she distributed paddy, rice, cocoanuts and a vast variety of other articles procured from the wilderness. (Rajavali p. 174.)

The followers having dressed the rice and victuals and having served them to the prince, the whole of them also feasted thereon She likewise having partaken of the residue of the meal bestowed on her by the prince, excited to the utmost pitch of delight, transformed herself (into a girl) of sixteen years of age; and decorating her person with innumerable ornaments, lovely as Maranga herself, and approaching him quickly inflamed the passion of the chief. Thereupon she caused a splendid bed curtained as with a wall and fragrant with incense to spring up at the foot of a certain tree. Seeing this procedure and foreseeing all the future advantages that were to result to him he passed the night with her. There, his seven hundred followers on that night slept outside the curtain surrounding their sovereign. This (destined) ruler of the land while reposing with the yakkhini hearing the sounds of song and music, inquired of the yakkhini regarding the same. Thereupon she being desirous of conferring the whole sovereignty on her lord replied, "I will render this Lanka habitable for men. In the city Siriwastha (Laggale in Uva) in this Island there is a yakkho sovereign Kalaseno and in the yakkha city Lankapura or Laygale in Matale there is (another) sovereign. Having conducted Kaleseno's daughter (Pusamitta) to Siriwastha, her mother (Kondanamika) is now bestowing her at a marriage festival on the sovereign of Siriwastha (Forbes ii. p. 80. Mahawanso. p. 49.) From that circumstance there is a grand festival in an assembly of yakkhos. That great assemblage will keep up that revel without intermission for seven days. This revel of festivity is in that quarter. Such an assemblage will not occur again. Lord! in this very day extirpate the yakkhos." Hearing this advice of hers the monarch replied to her; "Charmer of my affections! how can I destroy yakkhos, who are invisible?" "Prince," replied she, "placing myself in the midst of those yakkhos I will give a shout. On that signal fall to blows: by my supernatural power they shall take effect on their bodies." This prince proceeding to act accordingly destroyed the yakkhos. The Rajavali (p. 174) says that Kuveni transformed herself into a mare and the prince rode on her to the destruction of the yakkhos. The king having put (Kalaseno), the chief of the yakkhos to death, assumed his (court) dress. The rest of his retinue dressed themselves in the vestments of the other yakkhos. After the lapse of some days departing from the capital of the yakkhos and founding the city called "Tamba-panni." Wijayo settled there.

When the yakkhini had borne the prince two children he sent for a princess from Pandi. The prince receiving the announcement of the arrival of this royal maiden and considering it impossible that the princess could live with him at the same time with the yakkhini, he thus explained himself to Kuveni. "A daughter of royalty is a timid being; on that account leaving the children with me depart from my house." She replied, "on your account, having murdered yakkhos I dread these yakkhos: now I am discarded by both parties, whither can I betake myself?" Within my dominions (said he) to any place thou pleasest, which is unconnected with the yakkhos, and I will maintain thee with a thousand bali offerings." She who had been thus interdicted (from re-uniting herself with the yakkhos) with clamorous lamentation taking her children with her, in the character of an inhuman being, wandered to that very city (Lankapura) of inhuman inhabitants. She left her children outside the yakkha city. A yakkho who detested her recognizing her in her search for a dwelling went up to her. Thereupon another fierce yakkho among the enraged yakkhos (asked) "Is it for the purpose of again and again spying out the peace we enjoy that she is come?" In his fury he killed the yakkhini with a blow of his open hand. Her uncle a yakkho (named Kumaro) happening to proceed out of the yakkha city, seeing these children outside the town, "whose children are ye?" said he. Being informed "Kuveni's" he said "your mother is murdered, if ye should be seen here they would murder you also: fly quickly." Instantly departing thence they repaired to the (neighbourhood of the) Sumanta mountain. The elder having grown up married his sister and settled there. Becoming numerous by their sons and daughters, under the protection of the king they resided in that Malaya district. This person (Jiwahatto) retained the attributes of the yakkhos.—(Mahawanso pp. 47, 52.)

---

Asoko employed two yakkhos to assemble the priests throughout the whole of India and these messengers performed the task in seven days.

---

Two slaves who had been put to death transformed themselves into yakkhos and watched over the destiny of Pandukabhayo while he was yet a child in his mother's womb. And when he became man he was assisted by a certain yakkhini named Chetiyo (the widow of Jutindharo a yakkho who had fallen in the battle at Siriwasthapura). This yakkhini had the form and countenance of a mare and dwelt near the marsh of Tumbariungona at the Dhumarakkho mountain. A certain person in the prince's retinue having seen this beautiful (creature) white with red legs announced the circumstance to the prince (Pandukabhayo) saying, "There is a mare of such a description." The prince set out with a rope to secure her. She seeing him approach from behind, losing her presence of mind, from fear, under the influence of his imposing appearance fled without being able to exert the power she possessed of rendering herself invisible. He gave chase to the fugitive. She, persevering in her flight, made the circuit of that marsh seven times. She made three more circuits of the marsh and then plunged into the river at the Kachchakka ferry. He did the same and (in the river) siezed her by the tail; and at the same time grasped the leaf of a palmyra tree which the stream was carrying down. By his supernatural good fortune this (leaf) became an enormous sword. Exclaiming "I put thee to death," he flourished the sword over her. "Lord!" replied she to him, "subduing this kingdom for thee, I will confer it on thee: spare my life." Seizing her by the throat and with the point of the sword boring her nostril he secured her with his rope: she (instantly) became tractable. Conducting her to the Dhumarakkho mountain he obtained a great accession of warlike power by making her his battle steed. There, at the Dhumarakkho mountain he maintained his position for four years. Departing from thence with his forces he repaired to the mountain Arittho. There preparing for the impending war he remained seven years.

The prince having consulted with the yakkhini, in conformity with her advice he sent forward a strong party (in the character of a deputation), placing in their charge his insignia of royalty as well as the usual offerings made as a tribute and his martial accoutrements; and enjoined them to deliver this message (from him): "Take all these things: I will come to ask your forgiveness."

When this party had reached its destination, shouting "I will capture them forcing their camp," mounting his yakkha mare and surrounded by his whole army the prince threw himself into the midst of the fight. The yakkhini set up a loud shout. His (the prince's) army without as well as (the deputation) within (the enemy's camp) answered with a tremendous roar. The whole of the prince's army having slaughtered many of the enemy's men as well as the eight uncles, they made a heap of their (decapitated) heads. (Mahawanso, pp. 63—64.)

After his victory the prince established the yakkho Kalawelo in the eastern quarter of the city; and the chief of the yakkhos, Chitto, he established on the lower side of the Abhaya tank. He established the slave, born of the yakkho tribe, who had formerly rendered him great service, at the eastern gate of the city. He established within the royal palace itself the mare-faced yakkhini. He provided annually demon offerings and every other requisite for these four yakkhos. And in the days of public festivity, this monarch seated on a throne of equal eminence with the yakkho chief, Chitto, caused joyous spectacles representing the actions of the devos as well as of mortals to be exhibited, and delighting in the happiness and festivities (of his people) he was exceedingly gratified. (Mahawanso, pp. 64—65,)

He provided a nigrotha tree for the (devata) Wessawano and a temple for the Wiyadhodno; a gilt hall for his own use as well as a palace distributed into many appartments. These he constructed near the western gate. He employed a body of five hundred chandalas (low caste people) to be scavengers of the city, and two hundred chandalas to be nightmen; one hundred and fifty chandalas to be carriers of corpses and the same number of chandalas at the cemetery.

This monarch befriending the interest of the yakkhos, with the co-operation of Kalawelo and Chitto who had the power (though yakkhos) of rendering themselves visible (in the human world) conjointly with them, enjoyed his prosperity.

---

A certain yakkho called Panchako together with his wife Harita and five hundred youths attained Sowan (the first stage of sanctification, at the preaching of Majjantiko, who then thus addressed his converts. "Do not hereafter, as formerly, give way to pride of power and vindictive anger; but evincing your solicitude for the happiness of living creatures abstain from the destruction of crops: extend your benevolence towards all living creatures;

live, protecting mankind. They who had been thus exhorted by him, regulated their conduct accordingly.

---

In those days, as soon as an infant was born a marine monster emerging from the Ocean devoured it and disappeared. At the particular period (of this mission) a prince was born in a certain palace. The inhabitants seeing the priests and taking them to be emissaries of this rakkhasi, arming themselves surrounded them for the purpose of destroying them. The theros having ascertained what their object was thus addressed them: "We are pious ministers of religion and not the emissaries of the rakkhasi." The monster with her train at this instant emerged from the Ocean. Hearing of this (visitation) the concourse of people gave a grand shout of horror. The theros causing (by their power of working miracles) another band of terrifying monsters to spring up, of double that numerical power, surrounded the rakkhasi and her train on all sides. She, concluding this land has been appropriated by these, terrified fled.

---

When the first missionaries of Buddha landed in Ceylon a certain devo, who dwelt on a mountain, being desirous of exhibiting the theros, having assumed the form of an elk stationed himself there (in that neighbourhood) grazing. The sovereign descrying him and saying "It is not fair to shoot him standing," sounded his bowstring: the elk fled to the mountain. The king gave chase to the fleeing animal. On reaching the spot where the priests were, the thero came in sight of the monarch; but the metamorphosed devo vanished. The thero conceiving that the king might be alarmed if many persons (of the mission) presented themselves, rendered himself alone visible. The sovereign on seing him was surprised. The thero said to him, "come hither "Tisso." From his calling him simply "Tisso," the monarch thought he must be a yakkho.

When these missionaries sounded the call for prayer in Ceylon, the terrestrial devos shouted in response, and their shouts ascended to the Brahma world. In consequence of that call a great congregation of devos assembled. In that assembly the thero propounded the samachitta suttan (or the discourse of Buddho "on concord in faith.") To an asankiya of devos, superior grades of blessings of the religion were obtained. Innumerable nagas and supannas obtained the salvation of the faith. As on the occasion of the preaching of the thero Sariputto, so on that of the thero Mahindo, there was a great congregation of devos.

At the commencement of this kappo, the first in order was the vanquisher Kakasandho, a divine sage, perfect master of all the doctrines of the faith, and a comforter of the whole world. This Mahamegho pleasure garden was then called Mahatittha. The city situated to the eastward on the farther side of the Kadambo river was called Abhayapura. The ruling sovereign there was "Abhayo," and at that time this island was called Ojadipo. In this land by the instrumentality of the Rakshasas (especially Punakkha) a febrile epidemic afflicted its inhabitants. Kakusandho impelled by motives of beneficence, for the purpose of effecting the conversion of its inhabitants and the establishment of the faith, (after) having subdued this calamity, accompanied by forty thousand of his sanctified disciples, repairing to this land through the air, stationed himself on the summit of Dewakuto (Adam's Peak).

The king and the inhabitants of the capital, observing this divine sage, effulgent by the rays of his halo, as well as the mountain illuminated by his presence, instantly repaired thither. The people having hastened thither for the purpose of making "bali" offerings to the devatas, conceived that the ruler of the world and his sacerdotal retinue were devatas. This king (Abhayo) exceedingly overjoyed, bowing down to this lord of munis and inviting him to take refection, conducted him to the capital. (Mahawanso pp. 88—89.)

Dammasoco assigned for the custody of the great bo-branch, eighteen personages of royal blood, eighteen members of noble families, eight of the brahama caste, and eight of the settha caste. In like manner eight of each of the agricultural and domestic castes, as well as of weavers and potters, and of all other castes: as also nagas and yakkhos. This delighter in donations, bestowing vases of gold and silver, eight of each, (to water the bo-branch with) embarking the great bo-branch in a superbly decorated vessel on the river (Ganges); and embarking likewise the high priestess, Sanghamitta, with her eleven priestesses, and the Ambassador Ariththo at the head (of the mission); (the monarch) departing out of his capital and proceeding (the river procession with his army) through the wilderness of wingha, reached Tamalitta on the seventh day.

The devos, nagas and men, (during this land progress) kept up splendid festivals of offerings (on the river), and they also reached (the port of embarkation) on the seventh day.

The waves were still round the vessel carrying the bo-tree. Flowers blossomed in the sea around it. There was heavenly music Devos made offerings. The nagas tried to get the bo-branch by magic. The priestess became a Supanna (Garuda) and terrified the nagas. She however gave them the loan of the bo-branch for seven days, after which time they brought it from their settlement and restored it to her.

---

A certain old woman had laid out some paddy to dry. The devo (who presides over elements), causing an unseasonable shower to fall, wetted her paddy. Taking the paddy with her she went and rang the bell. Satisfying himself that the shower was unseasonable, sending the old woman away and saying to himself "while a king rules righteously the rain ought to fall at seasonable periods;" in order that he might be inspired with the means of giving judgment in the case, Asoko consigned himself to the penance of abstinence. By the supernatural merits of the king the tutelar devo who accepted of his bali offerings, moved with compassion repairing to the four kings of devos (of the Chatumaharaja world) imparted this circumstance to them. They, taking him along with them submitted the case to Sakko. Sakko (the supreme devo) sending for the spirit who presides over the elements, enjoined the fall of showers at seasonable hours only. The tutelar devo of the king imparted this (behest) to the monarch. From that period during his reign no shower fell in the day time: it only rained at the termination of every week in the middle of the night, and the ponds and wells were everywhere filled.

---

In Elaro's reign, Nandimitto used to kill the irreverent damilos secretly and the devos rendered the corpses invisible.

---

Duthugamini is said to have had giants in his service, and his priests went to the world of the devos to bring him the plan of the heavenly palace. And the devos brought night after night and placed at his gate bricks enough to build a temple.

He caused Buddha's acts during his existence as Wessantara Raja to be depicted in detail, as well as (his history) from the period of his descent from Tusitapura, to his attaining buddhohood at the foot of the bo-tree. At the farthest point of the four sides of the relic receptacle, the four great (mythological) kings (Dattarattho, Wirulho, Werupakkho and Wessawanno) were represented: thirty-three devos and thirty-two princes: twenty-eight chiefs of yakkhos : above these again, devos bowing down with clapsed hands raised over their heads : still higher (others bearing) vases of flowers : dancing devos and chanting devos : devos holding up mirrors, as well as those bearing bouquets of flowers, devos carrying flowers, and other devos under various forms: devos bearing rows of boughs made of jewels: and among them (representations of) the "dhammachakko" rows of devos carrying swords, as also rows bearing refection dishes. (Mahawanso p. 182.)

---

Twelve kotis of gods and men obtained the sanctification of Arhat, and devatas from the 6 Dewalokas came in chariots to hear the priests' hymn. (Mahawanso p.p. 191 & 198.)

---

A certain yakkho well known under the appellation of "rattakkhi" (red eyed monster) visited this land and afflicted its inhabitants in various parts thereof with ophthalmia. People meeting each other would exclaim "His eyes are also red!" and instantly drop down dead; and the monster would without hesitation devour their (corpses). The raja having been informed of the affliction (of the people) in the depth of his wretchedness took the vows of the "attasil" order, in his cell of solitary devotion. The monarch vowed "I will not rise till I have beheld that (demon)." By the influence of his pious merits, the said monster repaired to him. Then rising, he inquired of him, "who art thou?" (The demon) replied "I am (the yakkho)" The raja thus addressed him: "why dost thou devour my subjects: cease to destroy them." The demon then said, "Let me have the people of one district at least" On being told, "It is impossible;" lowering his demand by degrees, he asked. "Give me then one village:" The raja replied, "I can give thee nothing but myself: devour me." "That is not possible" (said the demon) and intreated that "bali offerings should be made to him in every village." The ru'er of the land replying, "sadhu," and throughout the island having provided accomodation for him, at the entrance of every village caused "bali" to be offered to him. By this means the panic created by this epidemic was suppressed by the supreme of men, who was endowed with compassion in the utmost perfection, and was like unto the light which illuminated the land. (Mahawanso p.p. 230—231.)

---

A banished thero who came from India was well versed in the rights of the Chuta (demon faith).—(Mahawanso p. 232.)

---

The yakkho Kalawelo had a temple and the king built a thupo for it.—(Mahawanso p. 237.)

According to the Rajaratnacari and Rajavali there was one Rattes or Dala Raksha at Rohona who lived on human flesh in the reign of Sri Sanghabhodi 1. (A. D. 242—246.) The same authorities inform us that king Maha Sen (A. D. 275—302) employed both men and demons in making the Minhiri and other lakes.

The Rajavali says "after the war of Ravana, before the present or fourth Buddha appeared as such, Ceylon had been inhabited by demons for the space of one thousand eight hundred and forty-four years: but no human inhabitants during that time were in Ceylon.

---

## THE NAGAS.

Buddha's second visit to Ceylon is said to have been undertaken for the purpose of settling a dispute between two nagas, an uncle and nephew, who quarrelled about a gem set throne.

---

There was a naga-king whose age extended to a kappo and who had seen 4 Buddhos. King Asoko sent a golden chain and having brought him placed him under the white canopy of dominion and seated him on a royal throne. Then Asoko and 16,000 women of his palace made offerings of flower to this nago-king who then miraculously caused an image of Buddho to appear before them. (Mahawanso p. 27.)

---

At that time a savage naga-king named Aravalo, who was endowed with supernatural powers, caused a furious deluge to descend, which was submerging all the ripened crops in Kasmira aud Gandhara. The said thero Majjhantiko, instantly repairing thither through the air and alighting on the lake Aravalo walked absorbed in profound meditation, on the surface of the water. The nagos seeing him, enraged (at his presumption), announced it to their king. The infuriated naga monarch endeavoured in various ways to terrify him: a furious storm howled and a deluge of rain poured down accompanied by thunder; lightning flashed in streams, thunder bolts (descended) carrying destruction in all directions, and high-peaked mountains tottered from their very foundation.

The nagos assuming the most terrific forms and surrounding him endeavoured to intimidate him. He himself (the naga king) reviling him in various ways spat smoke and fire at him. The thero by his supernatural power averted all these attempts to terrify him, and displaying his omnipotence thus addressed the nago monarch: "O naga ruler ! even if the devos were to unite with the (human) world to strike terror into me their efforts would prove negatory. Nay, if uplifting the whole earth together with its ocean and its mountains, thou wert to keep them on my head, even then thou wouldst fail to create in me an appalling terror. O, naga monarch, let thy destruction of the crops be arrested."

To him who had been subdued on hearing this reply the thero propounded his doctrines. Whereupon the naga king attained the salvation and state of piety of that faith.

In like manner in the Himawanta (or snowy) regions eighty four thousand nagas and many gandhabbos, yakkhos, and kumbhandakos (were converted).

Thereupon the naga king placing the thero on a gem-set throne, respectfully stood by, fanning him.

On that day the inhabitants of Kasmira and Gandhara, who had come with offerings to the naga king to appease his wrath and arrest the desolation of the crop, learning the supernatural character of the thero, bowing down to him instead of the naga king, stood reverentially at his side. (Mahawanso p. 73.)

---

It is not vouchsafed to the nagas to attain the four superior grades of sanctification: it is quite right therefore to remove the relics to a place where the four superior grades of sanctification are attainable. (Mahawanso p. 188.)

---

On a certain day, the king, while proceeding along the high road, mounted on his elephant, to bathe at the Pisso tank, saw, in the neighbourhood of Puttabhayo wiharo a mahanago on a white ant's hill stretched out straight as a pole and extended on his back, suffering from some internal complaint. On perceiving this, the monarch thought, "Surely this naga is suffering from some disease; and descending from his state elephant, and approaching the distressed mahanago thus addressed him—"Mahanago! it is only on the road that I became aware of thy case. Thou art unquestionably highly gifted, but as thou art also addicted to fits of rage on sudden impulses, on that account it is impossible for me to approach thee and treat thy complaint. Yet without approaching thee I can effect nothing. What is to be done. On being thus addressed, the hooded monarch, cobra de capello, thoroughly pacified, inserting his head alone into a hole in the ant hill, extended himself. Then approaching him and drawing his instrument from its case, he opened the naga's stomach and extracting the diseased part and applying an efficacious remedy he instantly cured the snake.

Casie Chetty, in his Gazetteer, p. 169, says, that in the Island of Nainativu, near Jaffna, there is a Hindu Temple sacred to Nagathambiran or the god of serpents, in which is a number of cobra de capellos that are daily fed by the Pandarams.

Poocke in his "India in Greece" makes certain observations on some of the semi-human beings, believed to have been in existence by the Greeks and the Romans, which, *mutatis mutandis*, will apply to the beings now under consideration.

"The Serpent, the Eagle, the Sun, are simply and ordinarily the serpent-tribe, eagle-tribe, sun-tribe.

"The Kentaurs (Centaurs) were Kandhaurs or emigrants from Kandhar.

"The Ophienses are the Afghans. The term aphiensa "Serpent-tribe," or snake-tribe is but reflected Sanscrit of aphgana.

"The term Amazons will be found to have no more connexion with the idea of breastless females than that of the Autochtons with the earth. The Amazons were plainly and simply "uma-soons," the daughters of Uma Uma is the appellative of Parvathi or Durga. That not only female Government existed of old but that large bodies of women adopted the use of arms will now be set beyond a doubt.

"The same system of personification sank deep into the Hindoo Cosmogony, and in fact the whole of what is called their mythology. The Cabeiri are, as Wilford has endeavoured to prove, Cuvera, the Hindu god of wealth and regent of the North,—that is, in simple language, the Khyber; its region is wealthy and abounds with rubies; gold is found in the rivers in its vicinity, and it was likewise the ruling northern power in those early days. The Hindoos, like the Greeks, have their own derivation for Cuvera; and alluding to the deformity of the god, who is represented as having three legs and eight teeth, they derive his name from *Cu, vile*, and, *vera, a body*. Here then, the Cuvera of the Hindus, the Pataikoi of the Phœnicians, the Cabeiri of the Greeks, are simply distorted records and distorted comments upon the plain facts of Budhist worship, Budhist industry and Budhist wealth, abounding in the regions of the Kheaibar and its relative vicinity."

Regarding the mythical period of Singhalese history the Chinese author

FaHian (A. D. 400) as quoted by Tennent, vol. I. p. 335, says—"Before the advent of Wijayo the kingdom of lions was inhabited originally not by men but by demons and serpents. Merchants are attracted to the island by the prospect of trade, but the demons remained unseen, merely exposing the precious articles which they wished to barter, with the price marked for each, at which the foreign traders were at liberty to take them, depositing the equivalents indicated in exchange."

---

## KASI KANDAM.

Chapter 77 entitled the Kethara-lingkam. There was a devotee of Siva, of the name of Iraniyagarbha, who went to Ketharam and died there. The sanctity of the place was so great that his soul was instantly carried to heaven in a celestial chariot by the gods. His pupil Vathishdan, who lived at Benares, made it a point to visit the spot twice a day for worship. He became very old and was scarcely able to support himself on his staff, but he continued his visits as usual.

Siva took pity on him, and appearing in a dream said "old devotee! I am come to meet you here, you need not go there." The devotee replied "grant this great blessing not only to me, but to the whole world," Accordingly Siva established himself at the Pavakara thirtham in Benares.

---

## THIRU-VATHA-VURAR-PURANAM.

This is a poetical narrative of one of the 64 sports of Siva. It contains no information as to the date of its composition or of the events which it narrates. Nor does it mention any names of persons except that of Manikkavasakar, who, we know from other sources, lived at the end of the 10th century and in the reign of Arimardana Pandiyan. (Madura Sthalapuranam as quoted by Dr. Caldwell).

The 9th chapter of Thiruvatha-vurar-puranam is headed "The defeat of the Buddhists in controversy." The controversy is said to have occurred in this wise:

A Saivite went to Ceylon and obtruded the greatness of the god of Sithamparam or Tillai of the Chola country on the notice of the Buddhists. A Buddhist champion, a priest, set out from Ceylon boasting that he would establish Buddhism in Tillai. He held a public controversy at the golden Hall of the Temple of Tillai, with Manikka-vasakar for his opponent, but was ignominiously defeated. The kings of Chola and Ceylon who came to be present at the controversy met in a friendly manner; and the latter gave the former elephants and gems, being a part of the usual tribute which Ceylon paid to the Cholan. The king of Ceylon had a daughter, who was dumb; she was present at the controversy and her tongue was miraculously loosened at the prayers of Manikkavasakar. The king of Ceylon and all the Buddhists who were with him embraced Saivaism before their return to Ceylon.

---

## THE SKANDA-PURANAM.

(Tamil translation.)

### VINTHAKIRIPPADALAM.

Naratha, (the rishi whose special occupation, like that of Ate, is to create discord among the gods) roused the jealousy of the Vindia mountain by praising the greatness of the Maha Meru.

Vindia then raised itself up until it touched the heavens and incommoded the passage of the gods and the planets. Siva sent down Agastiar to subdue the mountain. As a provision for the way, Agastiar brought with him, for sacrificial use, one of the seven rivers of heaven, viz., the Ponni, enclosed in small vessel in which Siva enjoined her to remain until the rishi should motion her away with his hand. When Agastiar reached Vindia the mountain despised him for his uncouth and diminutive stature. But the rishi put his hand on the head of the proud mountain and pressed it down till its bottom reached the snake who bears the Earth. After performing other wonderful achievements, Agastiar took up his residence at Pothiya malai but it does not appear that he went further south.

About this time, Indra, the king of the gods, took the form of a bamboo-bush and was concealing himself in the midst of a garden for fear of the oppression of the Rakshasas. This garden was now dying for want of water. At the suggestion of Naratha, Indra prayed to Ganesha. Ganesha assumed the form of a crow and alighted on the brim of the vessel that contained the Ponni. The unsophisticated rishi raised the back of his hand in order to drive away the crow. The Ponni considered herself released by the motion; and she rose with all the grace and majesty of heaven, and proceeded on her way to the sea, watering, of course, the garden of Indra as she went along. Kaveri is the terrestrial name of the Ponni.

## VALLI-YAMMAI-THIRU-MANAP-PADALAM.

In Thondaimandalam there is a place called Etpadi. Near Etpadi is a mountain gloomy as the body of Vishnu. Its name is Kathiraimalai. Near it is a village of Vedars (hunters), whose chief adopted a foundling girl and named her Valli. The news of her great beauty having reached Scanda who was then encamped at Thanikai (near Madras), he came to the Veda village under the pretext that he wished to perform ablutions in the Sacred Sea of Cape Comorin. Having found opportunities to meet her alone, he persuaded her to run away with him. The fugitives were pursued by the Vedars and an encounter took place in which Scanda became victorious.

The Kathiraimalai mentioned here is identified with two different places. One at Thondaimandalam in India and the other with Katragama near Dondra in Ceylon. Our concern is only as respects Katragama, of which place and its temple much valuable information may be gathered from a brochure entitled "Katragama" published by Assistant Colonial Surgeon Covington at the Jaffna Patriot Office.

## THIRIKONASALAPURANAM.

This is a work of no small literary merit. Its author Mr. Masillamani Muttukumaru is a native of Trincomalie where he still lives. It consists of 1,591 stanzas divided into 20 chapters.

It is chiefly valuable as a collection of all the traditionary legends relating to the place.

Chapter IV.—Konaivaraippadalam. Ravanan's mother, a very old woman, who was a constant devotee of Siva, could not visit Siva's shrine on account of its distance. The son pitied her and wished to bring the god to where she was. So he cut the mountain on which the god dwelt and had nearly succeeded in severing it from its base, but the god caused Ravanan's sword to break in two and Ravanan himself to be precipitated into the sea. Determined to move by compassion what he could not by force, Ravanan began to mortify himself. He pulled out his eyes and offered them for sacrificial flowers. He cut off one of his heads, pulled out the muscles of his arms, and with the skull and the muscles made a stringed instrument, and sang the praises of Siva on it. Siva was now moved, and not only consented to allow himself and the mountain to be removed, but he cured Ravanan of the deformity which he had brought on himself. The gods, anxious to frustrate Ravanan's success, sent down Vishnu in the garb of a sacred devotee. The devotee persuaded Ravanan to believe that his mother was dead and made him perform the usual funeral ceremony, which whilst he performed, his mother actually died.

Chapter VI.—Agastiappadalam. As in the Kalveddu but more elaborately drawn.

Chapters IX-X. Vara Rama Thevar, king of Chola, came to Trincomalie.

On his return the queen conceived and brought forth a son who was named Kulakkoddan, from a horn that he had on his forehead. Kulakkoddan also visited the sacred mountain as his father had done before him and constructed the tanks Allaikkulam and Vendarayen Kaddu.

Chapters XII-XV.—Thiruk-kulang-kanda-padalam. In the city called Asoka-ma-nakaram in the country of Kalinga there reigned a king named Asoko-Suntharan. His queen's name was Manoka Sunthari. She brought forth a daughter having teeth, developed breasts, and long well arranged hair. By advice of astrologers the child is put into an ark and sent adrift on the ocean. She is picked up at Panawa by Manuneya Gajabahu of Anurajapura whom she afterwards succeeds under the name of Adaka Savunthari. She sends an army to drive away Kulakkoddan from Trincomalie but afterwards marries him. Kanthalai is constructed by demons (putham) and the god Ganesha is established on the bund. A colony is brought from Chola and planted at Thambalakamam and Kottiyapuram. Another colony of 30 families is brought from Marungkur, of 21 families from Karai, and, a ruler Thaniyunnap-pupalan from Madura. The king and queen visit the Tank and order the building of the Pendukal kaddu. Thence the royal pair visit Thambalakamam and Trincomalie.

On their return to Anurajapura the queen gives birth to Raja Singhan. The king visits Trincomalie alone and is absorbed in the deity.

Chaps. XVI—XIX. Buveneka Gajabahu of the solar race abandons Saivaism and becomes a Buddhist. He procures the white Banian of Indra and plants it at Anurajapura, which place is thence named Vellarasu-nadu, the white Banian country

There was a fight between the servants of the Trincomalie Temple and some Budhists, in which the latter were defeated. When the king heard of it he was highly enraged and marched with his army with the intention of destroying the temple.

On the way he loses his eye-sight, but Siva appears to him in the form of an aged Brahman and restores his sight. Hence the place where he experienced the miracle is called Kanthalai up to the present day, i. e. eye-cure. He becomes a devotee of Siva and enlarges the privileges and incomes of the temple. After his return to Anurajapura, Pararasa Singhan, Nalan and other kings visit Trincomalie. In latter days the temple was neglected and foreign kings began to rule over Trincomalie in the place of the pupalar.

Chapt. XX. Thisaiyukkira Cholan's daughter Maruthappiravika Valli had the face of a horse. She visited Mantotte, Thirukkethichchuram, Palavi, Kanniya, Trincomalie, the Mahaveli, Karasai, Verukal, Thirukkovil, Kathirai, the Manikka river, Sengkadakanakari and Nakulamalai, in which last place she was cured of her deformity. She married Ukkira Sena Singkan and gave birth to Vara Rasa Singkan at Choli. This Vara Raja Singkan came to Ceylon, occupied the throne of Langka, married the Pandiyan's daughter, Samathuthi, and reigned from Sengkadaka nakari. He built the shrine of Thambalakamam and transferred the deity thither from Trincomalie.

---

## YALPANACH-CHARITHTHIRAM.

The history of the kings who reigned over Langka and who shall hereafter reign over it, with an account of the colonization of the Island.

In the beginning of the Kali Yuga, Ravana was king of Ceylon. He carried away Sita, the beatiful wife of Rama captive. Her husband invaded Ceylon with an army of monkeys, killed the ravisher and bestowed the kingdom on Vibhishana. On his way back he established the Sivalingkam at Ramaseram and returned to Oude. A lutist who was in the pay of Vibhishana found his way to the court of Oude and begged for a royal prince, alleging that he had planted a colony of a 1000 families in the northern part of Ceylon called Manattidal and that a king was wanted to rule over it. A son of Kulakethu, the maiththunan of Rama, set out with the lutist, reached Manattidal, changed its name into Yalpanam and reigned under the name of Kulangkai

Ariyach Chakkirawarththi. This was about the year 3000 of the Kaliyuga. This king's father-in-law was Thisaiyukkira Cholan whose son Ramarasa had a son of the name of Singka Kethu. Singka Kethu came to Ceylon with his sister Maruthappiravikavalli. This lady had a deformity of which she was cured by bathing in the Kirimalai stream. The brother and sister then visited Kathiramalai and on their return home passing througl Jaffna again,.the prince Ukkirama Sena Singkan married the princess. The offspring of this marriage was a prince who had a leonine face and a tail. Vibhishana, who long reigned over Ilam, sent for this prince, named him successor with the title of Jeya thungka Vira Vararaja Singhan, and departed this life. Jeyathungkavira Vararajesingkan sent for and married Singka Kethu's daughter Samathuthi of Chola, who came accompanied by 60 Vanniyar. These 60 Vanniar were allowed to form settlements in Adangkappattu i.e. a division "independent" of Jaffna and Langkapuram. One of the Vanniyar remained behind and became a Thisai (Dissava) to King Desaratha Vira Vararasa Singhan. The Adangakppattu was then under the Chandar and Fishers: Karikkaddumulai under the Paraiyar: Thannikkal in Metpattu under the Vedar: The East and the North corners under the Puthar and Rakshasas who had concealed themselves there at the invasion by Rama: Cheddikulam under the Parangki Carlo and others of his race: the uncultivated parts Thambalakam, Kottiapuram, Batticaloa, &c., under barbers.

The 59 Vanniar sent for men from Madura, Tondamandalam, Karaikkal, Trichinoppali, Kudalur, Marungkur, and there came from these places the poor among all classes: the Vellalar, Brahmans, Shoemakers, Malayalis, Akampadis, Thimilar, Potters and Christians. They were led by the chiefs Ilagnchingka Mappanan, Allavaku, Aththimappanan, Singka Mappanam and others [who are named with their places of settlement both in Jaffna and the Vannis.] With the aid of these new comers the Vanniyar overcame the original inhabitants, became kings in their place, but paid tribute to Jaffna,

Five of these Vanniyar went to Madura and drove the Parangkis from thence, and on their return, divided the Vannis among themselves. Hence the name 5 Provinces. This happened in Kaliyuga 3420.

Mannar took its name from the verb "mannukirathu," to tuck up one's clothes, from the circumstance that the women of that place tucked up their clothes and got into the water in their eagerness to follow Rama when he crossed over to the main land of Ceylon.

The Thulukkar (Turks i. e. Mahommedans) under their leader Mera, and the Mukkuvar under their chief Vediarasan infested the seas and committed piracies. At that time Kannakai the daughter of Manakar of Madura was about to be given in marriage to Kovalan the son of Masaththa and her father wrote to the Cholan for nakaratnams (i. e. Snake Gems.)

The Cholan dispatched an expedition under a Kurukula captain to go to Ceylon and procure the gems. This captain defeated the Mukkavar and the Thulukkar, of whom the first went to Batticaloa and formed a settlement at Ilanthaikkadu, while the other took refuge at Vidattaltivu.

Alliarasani the daughter of the king of Pandi had a number of Paravar in her employ to fish for pearls. Some of these Paravar, while carrying in their vessels Vira Rasan, a chetty, and his wealth, were driven on the shores of Ceylon by stress of weather. They landed and built cities at Kuthiramalai, Silavaththurai and Chilaw under the auspices of the chetty. Afterwards the chetty moved on to Chettikulam in the Adangkkappattu, opened the tank Valai and built the temple of Santhirasekaran. This happened in the year of the Kali yuga 3348. It was after this, the place was called Chetty-kulam and the Parangkis took possession of it viz. in 3390.

Vala Singka-aradchi brought Mullai malanar, Sarukumalanar, and Sivanallamalanar from Trichinopalli and settled in Mullivalai nadu which was governed by the Chandar and the Fishers. The Aradchi had seven daughters all of whom became recluses and founded 60 holy places and wells.

The Vanniyar now thought of returning to Madura but on their way they suffered shipwreck and were drowned in the sea. Their wives, the Vannichchimar, in the mean time arrived in Ceylon with very large retinues including Christians, and learning the fate of their husbands, 54 of them mounted the funeral pyre. One went to join her husband in Kandi, and the remaining five went to the five provinces of their husbands and rulod over them taking each a new husband, who was simply styled Ayinthi and had no, share in the government. When these Vannichchimar were dead, their provinces were ruled by Ilagnchingkamappanan's son Thisaiyvilangka Mappanan. After this a younger son of the Vanniyan who was Desava went to Marungkur and married Kurisi the daughter of Jayethunga Vanniyan. His name was Innathiththbian. Collecting an army on the continent, he came and took possession of all the Vannis. This was in the year 3996. At this time Kanaka-chakkrawarthi, a descendant of Kulangkaich-chakkrawarthi, was king of Jaffna. He was visited by Supathisda Muni, the son of Agastia Muni. Supathishda prophesied and said "In the days of your children Pararasa Sekaran, Sekarasa Sekaran and Sangkili, the last will join the Parangkis and destroy his brothers. The Parangkis will afterwards fall out with him, and losing a battle with them he will kill himself and his horse; and the Parangkis will become supreme lords on the 15th of Vaiyasi in 5647. They will reign 40 years, oppressing Saivaism and will establish Christianity. Then Ulanthes will take the kingdom on the 20th of Paingkuni 5687, reduce the Vannis also, and will reign with justice. On the 3rd of Ani 5794 the English king will overcome the Dutch and will take Kandi in 5800, but will lose a large number of his soldiers. Afterwards on the 6th of July 5875 the Dutch and the French will overcome the English by stratagem. And after that, Puloka Singha Raja Singha, son of the king of Ketharam, will conquer all countries on the north and south including Ceylon and other places in 5994. According to this prophecy things are happening.

Pararajasingkan has concealed his treasures in Muthalianka llu. So say the great, the Munis, Vaya, Copper books and Kelveddu. Note, the past history is also in Kelveddu. [*Note by the translator* —The above is a work of no authority. It is a confusion of persons, places, dates and events.]

---

## PUTHATHTHAMPI NADAKAM.

Nadakam is drama. The distinction into comedies and tragedies does not obtain in Tamil. Generally-speaking in all dramatical compositions there are a birth, marriage and death. But there is no drama without a scene of the endurance of unmerited evil or a scene of female devotion. Nor is there one which ends without poetical justice being done to all parties.

The author of the present Nadakam is, as is stated in it, one Davidu, son of Juvan Costan of Mantotte. But he gives us neither the date of his work: nor that of the events which he dramatises. The latter date however is easily found. The Vinea Taprobanea (page 94) says that Rev. Caldero was decapitated in the year A.D. 1658 by the Dutch on a charge of his having concealed his knowledge of the treasonable correspondence which Don Lewis Puthaththampi had with the Portuguese. The year 1658 (June 21st) was the date when the Dutch took the fortress of Jaffnapatanam from the Portuguese.

Puthaththampi and his dramatist appear from this work to have been Saivites notwithstanding the Christian names they bore. For the dramatist invokes on his work the favour of the usual Hindu gods, and represents his hero as appealing to the same gods for succour in times of distress, while he carefully makes the Dutch characters swear like Christians.

The events of the drama are as follow:—

The Dutch Viceroy of Colombo sent Anthony Amral as Governor of Jaffna and one Andirado, a man of the Kurukula caste as Amral's Muthaliar. Amarl appointed Puthaththampi, a Velalan of the Karala section, as second Muthaliar, and one Sinne Ulanthes as Captain of the Fort. Andirado made improper advances to Puthaththampi's wife, which she not merely rejected, but subjected Andirado's messengers to a degrading punishment. In order to avenge himself, Andirado had a letter framed purporting to have been written by Puthaththampi and Sinne Ulanthes and directed to Kirthi-singkan king of Kandi, offering to betray the country to him. The letter was of course intercepted, and its bearer acted his part exactly as had been arranged. Puthaththampi was condemned on the strength of this letter and was, by the procurance of Andirado, executed without a moment's respite. Sinne Ulanthes was then absent at Kayts building the sea-fortress. On his return he learnt the fate of Puthaththampi and, for fear of falling by an unjust sentence, committed suicide. But Puthaththampi's brother-in-law Kayilayappillai, Vanniyan of Kachchaitturai, went to Colombo and made a representation to the Viceroy, upon which both Anthony Amral and Andirado were ordered to go to Colombo to defend themselves. On the way, Amral wilfully threw himself into the sea and was drowned, Andirado was killed by an elephant at Musali or Pandaraththarthoppu. Puthaththampi left behind a widow, and a son named Sothi-nathan. The widow committed suicide through grief.

*Note by the translator.*—Ribeyro makes mention of an Anthonio Amral de Menezes, a Portuguese Governor of Mannar who was killed by a shot from an arquebuse in 1658. This loss so dispirited the Portuguese that although their number was large, they took fright and all fled to Jaffnapatam; and the Dutch possessed themselves of Mannar (Lee's Translation p. 51.) In 1658 Adrian Van Der Meyden was the Dutch Governor of Colombo. Our author seems to be so ignorant a man that he uses the name Amral probably on the principle that all steamers are known to the vulgar in Ceylon by the name

"Pearl", as "Pearl" was the name of the first steamer they were acquainted with.

---

## THE VINEA TAPROBANEA.

This is a very accurate and interesting compilation, giving an account of Christianity in Ceylon from the beginning of the 16th to the end of the 18th century. It was made by the late Philip Canjamanadan, Shroff Muthaliar of the Colombo Customs, from, as he explains in his preface, Cosmas, Nicephoras, Dorotheus, Ribeiro, Baldeus, Knox, Cordiner, Hardward, Philalethes, Bohours, Dorego, and other early writers. He has also added a few well established traditions collected by himself. The work was published in 1855. Notwithstanding the Latin name it bears, it is written in Tamil prose and the compact terseness of its style renders a summary impossible. We shall only notice here such parts of it as illustrate the Vaipavamalai.

In the year 1543 the inhabitants of the Island of Mannar, moved by grace, invited St. Francis Xavier to come over from Trivendram where he then was. Being unwilling to leave his infant congregation, he sent word to a preacher whom he had stationed at Tutucorin, to accept the invitation in his place. That preacher went to Mannar accordingly and converted many persons to Christianity.

The king of Jaffna, to whom Mannar belonged at the time, was a staunch Saivite and began to persecute the converts. He imprisoned, starved and maimed them. He confiscated their property and used many other oppressive measures. Finding these unavailing, he took to killing them. Of the Kadayar of Pesalai alone there fell 600 in this persecution, including women and children. He further proclaimed an order prohibiting the landing of Christian ministers within his territories. Nevertheless Christianity made such progress that his two sons and a sister of his and her son became converts. The eldest son suffered martyrdom by order of his inhuman father. But the second son and the nephew escaped to Goa. So did the king's eldest brother, the lawful sovereign of Jaffna, whose rights the tyrant had usurped and set a price on his head.

When Xavier learnt the state of things, he landed at Mannar but returned soon after to Negapatam where his presence was urgently required. He landed again at Mannar in 1548. Among his first converts were an exiled royal family of Kandi, of whom the king took the name of Don Philip, and his infant daughter Dona Catharina. The same year Xavier visited Jaffna and having successfully induced the king to send an embassy to the Portuguese to court their friendship, he himself accompanied the embassy and set out to Goa on the 20th of March, 1548. The embassy returned with a favourable answer but the king had in the mean time changed his mind, and when the Portuguese attempted to build a church, he drove them out of his kingdom, from a fear that they were going to build a fort, and began his persecution afresh. Xavier shook the dust off his feet and left Ceylon for China where he closed his eventful life in 1552 in the city of Canton.

In 1551 the king of Trincomalie died, leaving his infant son as his successor. When the boy was 8 years of age an enemy arose and usurped his kingdom. His friends sent him to Tutucorin for safety. There he embraced the Christian faith, and his followers, forty in number, copied his example. By this step he gained the good will of the Parava Christians of Tutucorin, who armed themselves on behalf of their royal convert, proceeded to Trincomalie and made war upon the usurper but were completely defeated.

In the year 1581, Pope Gregory XIII having adjusted the errors of the Julian Calendar, the adjustment was introduced into Ceylon. Accordingly 10 days were omitted in the month of October of that year, so that, the 5th of that month was read as the 15th.

In 1590 the Portuguese wrested Mannar from the king of Jaffna, and in the following year they advanced on his capital, defeated him, and slew him with his oldest son in his very palace. The whole kingdom of Jaffna thus became a part of the Portuguese territory. But it did not remain long under them. In 1593 it was taken from them by Don Juvan Vimala Dharma of Kandi and it remained as a province of Kandi till 1620, when it was again taken by the Portuguese. In 1626 the Kandiyan King sent Senaviratna Attapattu Muthaliar with a well appointed army to retake Jaffna but the army was completely routed and was pursued until it reached Kandi.

In 1658 Mannar and Jaffna fell into the hands of the Dutch. Under the Portuguese the fort of Mannar contained 150 Europeans and 200 natives: and the district of Mannar was divided into seven parishes, Sithathi, Thoddaveli, Karusal, Erukkalampiddi, St. Pedro, Pesali, and Thalaimannar The town of Jaffna had an almshouse and a hospital, and a population of 200 soldiers, 300 Europeans and 400 natives. On its west side there were a Franciscan monastery and a church, on the south a Dominican monastery and a church, and on the east a Jesuite monastery and a church. The district of Jaffna was divided into five pattus which contained 32 parishes with a church in each parish.

---

*Valikama pattu* 14.

| | | |
|---|---|---|
| 1. Tellipallai | 2. Mallakam | 3. Mayiliddi |
| 4. Achchuveli | 5. Uduvil | 6. Vaddukkoddai |
| 7. Pandaththerippu | 8. Changkani | 9. Manippay |
| 10. Nallur | 11. Vannarpannai | 12. Chundikkuli |
| 13. Kopay | 14. Puththur | |

*Thenmaradchip pattu* 5.

| | | |
|---|---|---|
| 1. Navatkuli | 2. Chavakachcheri | 3. Kachchai |
| 4. Varani | 5. Eluthumadduval. | |

*Vadamaradchip pattu* 3.

| | | |
|---|---|---|
| 1. Kaddaiveli | 2. Uduppiddi | 3. Paruththiththurai |

*Puchchilaippalli pattu* 4.

1. Puloppalai 2. Mukamalai
3. Thampakamam 4. Mullippattu

*The Islands-pattu.*

1. Urkavatturai (Kayts) 2. Allappiddi 3. Valani
4. Karathivu 5. Punkuduthivu 6. Nayinathivu.

The district of Vanni consisted of the pattus of Punakari, Pallavarayankaddu, Perungkalli, Manthai, Nannaddan, Aripu and others, in each of which there was a church.

The priests of these distant pattus concealed themselves in the neighbouring Kandiyan territories, but those of Mannar and Jaffna, who numbered about 50, marched out of the fort of Jaffnapatam when it was taken by the Dutch, and were sent to India with the garrison.

---

## THE KALVEDDU.

Kalveddu literally means an inscription upon a rock. It is now applied to all records of remarkable events whether carved on stone or written on less durable substance. There is one relating to the temple of Isvaran of Trincomalie which is unquestionably a work of great antiquity, but it bears evident marks of having received additions from time to time up to very recent dates. The following is a brief summary of its contents.

" This work is composed partly in poetry and partly in prose by the poet Kavi-rasa-varothyan. It relates how Rama Deva, the son of Manu-nithi-kanda-Cholan of the solar race, visited Trincomalie, and after him his son Kulak-koddan came and repaired the temple and its towers, built the terraced halls, and made the sin-dispelling well. For the continuance of the service of Isvaran he brought 51 families from Karai and Marungkar in Chola ; and invited Thani-yunnap-pupalan of the lunar race (a Vanniyan from Madura) and appointed him king over the new colony. These he finished on Monday the 10th of Idapam in the year of Kali-yukam 512. And four vears afterwards he built the never failing tank and filled it with the water of the Mahavali ganga sufficient to irrigate a paddy-sowing-extent of 17,000 amunams "

Kulakkoddan lays down the duties of the temple and assigns a portion to each of the 51 families. His injunction to the Vanniyan is given thus:

" Take life for life, for less heinous offences, imprisonment, stocks and lashes. If dancing girls commit an offence, exact a penalty of cocoanuts ; in the case of other women, lash them or make them carry loads of sand according to rank. Forsake not the law of Manu. Anger is sin. Your neighbour's wife is your mother. Follow truth, eschew falsehood. Do no evil, help the poor, do not give way to pride. Beside the tax of the lands which I have planted and given to the people, I assign the customs-dues also to the temple."

Kulakkoddan's prophecy.

" A time will come in the distant future when the services of the temple will be neglected. But Gajabahu from Anurajapuram will dedicate more lands to the temple and restore its services to their original glory. After a long interval, the services will be transferred to Kalanimalai owing to the incursions of the Parangkis. The Parangkis will be overcome by the Hollander. The leonine solar dynasty of Ceylon will then be diminished. The Vadukan (Tamil) will reign over all Ceylon, but the Hollanders will snatch a small portion of his territory from him. A new power will overthrow the Hollanders and befriend the Vadukar, and the two friendly powers will restore the worship of the temple. After this, will come Singkam to govern the whole Ceylon. [Here follows a description of the various works which Kulakkoddan executed ]

### Death of Kulakkoddan.

After the most solemn warning to the people to keep up the services of the temple, he went into the holy of holies and was absorbed into the deity. Sivan's revelation to his wife when Trincomalie was originally formed by the fall of the sacred peak is given in the following words.

"When the first three ugas are past and the fourth is come, then will the Feringees endanger Sivasamayam but will themselves be over-thrown by Raja Singkam (the Royal Lion.) This king will invite the Hollanders and request them to finish the conquest of the sea ports. And the faithless Hollanders will conquer them but keep them for 140 years. A new king will come to help, will destroy the Hollanders and restore all the ports to the king of Ceylon. And there will be peace".

---

### The arrival of Puvineya Gaja Baku.

"Gajabaku came as had been predicted by astrologers. At his approach the priests of the temple died through fear, and the sacrifices were stopped for seven Nalikai. Two new priests came miraculously from the ocean and the king gave them 1,100 pons to revive the interrupted sacrifices and increased the income of the temple by the tithes of a territory bounded on the north by Karampakam, on the west by Munnichchuram, on the south by Sangkamankandi, on the east by the sea of Bengal".

The rest of the work is in prose and contains an account of the nine gems presented to the temple by nine different kings and the custodians appointed to take care of them. It next details the duties of the various classes of the officers of the temple

---

### Death of Puvineya Gaja Baku.

Going from Trincomalie this king repaired the temple of Munnichchuram and added to it the temple of Thiruk-Kailesar. He afterwards returned to his capital and died, leaving the kingdom to his son Manuneya-Gaja-Baku.

Then follow the arrival of Nalach-chakkra-warththi of Nidatha-thesam and his presents to the temple.

---

## Gaja Baku's Prophecy.

"Para-rasa-Sekaran and Seka-rasa-Sekaran, kings of the country lying to the north of Trincomalie, will next come and present valuable gifts and the land Thiriya-vur to the temple. And after them will come one of their successors to their kingdom, named Ariyarasan, who will also present many valuable gifts".

Here follow accounts of other gifts, the arrival of new officers for the temple, the riches of the temple, the place where the same were deposited, and, among other things, a caldron of Senthuram (a powder) for transmuting iron into gold.

The next is an account of Kalani-malai:

"To witness the marriage of Sivan with Parvathi, the sentient beings of all the universe flocked to Kayilasam, the Silver mountain, the residence of Sivan. Akastiyar also proceeded thither. When he reached Kalanimalai, a mountain within a distance of three kathams from Kayilasam, the world lost its balance and the north began to sink and the south to rise. To adjust the balance, Akastiyar was sent back to the south. He came and established himself at this Kalanimalai which also is three kathams distant from the southern Kayilasam (Trincomalie). He established a Siva lingam at Karasai on the banks of the Mahavali ganga which flows from Samanayangkiri. Here he was vouchsafed with a sight of the marriage ceremonies and all the festivities as if in a panorama"

## THE CONSTRUCTION OF THE HOLY TANK (GANTALAWE. DANTALAWE OR KANTHALAI.)

"On the northern continent, there is a country called the Kalingkathesam. To the north of that country is situated the town Somakiri at a distance of 21 kathams. One of the kings of that town was Asoka Suntharan of the solar race. His wife, Manoka Sunthari, gave birth to a female child that came from the womb with a well arranged head of hair, a full set of teeth and a pair of fully developed breasts. Hence her name Munmulaiththadakai i. e., Thadakai, having breasts prematurely. By the advice of astrologers, the king put the child into an ark and sent it adrift on the ocean. It was picked up by Manu-neya-gaja-baku of Ceylon, near the present village of Panakai, (properly Palanakai, i.e., "child-smile", because the child smiled when it was taken out of the ark). The child was taken to the capital Unnasakiri (Hunusgiri) and adopted by the king as his daughter. When she grew up she succeeded her adoptive father on the throne under the name of Adaka Sunthari. During her reign Kulakkoddan came to Ceylon and busied himself with the restoration of these edifices. She sent her minister with an army to drive him out of the Island, but overcome with fear at the greatness of the enemy, the minister pretended that he was sent by the Queen to offer her services to him. Kulakkoddan was supernaturally informed of the true object of the mission, but he nevertheless accepted the offer and asked for advice and aid to construct a never failing tank. The minister said "there is a plain surrounded on three sides by a range of mountains and irrigated by 64 small tanks. Let us make the whole plain one large tank and it will irrigate all the land up to the sea-shore." Kulakkoddan approved of the suggestion. The minister brought one Putha-raja and six small puthams, deeming the work to be too small for a large number of puthams or for large sized puthams. The tank and a canal from the Mahavali-ganga, of 28 kathams, were completed in nine days;

during which, the seven puthams were fed at the rate of 21 amanams of rice with the usual accompaniments in proportion. The keys of the sluices of the tank were left in the custody of the Veda chief Veera Suriya Udaiyar.

---

### Marriage of Kulakkkoddan.

Kulakkoddan afterwards went to Unnasakiri and married the Queen. She came to see the tank, and finding one portion of the bund somewhat low, she got her women to repair it. That portion is called the Pendukal-kaddu i. e., women's bund.

The Queen gave birth to a son who had the face of a lion. After her death this son succeeded her on the throne under the name of Singka-Kumaran.

Here follows a long account of the original famlies brought from India and how they failed and how their places were filled by new colonies.

---

### The Portuguese.

Seventy five years after Ariyachchakkra-varththi's visit to Trincomalie, and when a Vannichchi had reigned 24 years, the Feringi disturbances arose.

---

### The Kayilaya Malai.

This is a poetical composition of no mean ability and was evidently designed to celebrate the praises of Seka-rasa-sekaran under the very thin disguise of celebrating the sanctity of the temple of Kayilaya Nathar of Nallur. The author was Muththurasan, son of Senthiyappan of Chola, who was no doubt a contemporary of the king.

" There is a Jampu or Naval tree to the south of the Maha-meru mountain. It gives name to one division of this world, namely the Navalan-thivu. The Navalan thivu is divided into nine continents of which the Paratha Kandam is one. And Ceylon is situated in Paratha-Kandam.

In times past the Cholan of the solar race, wearer of the Aththi-flower-garland, whose country is watered by the Kaveri, and whose banner displays the tiger, had a maiden daughter, who set out on a pilgrimage to visit sacred places. She was encamped near the Seathirththam of this Island with her attendants and a large army. The king of Ceylon, who had the face of a lion, stealthily carried her away by night to his capital Kathira-malai and made her his queen. She gave birth to a son of great personal beauty but having a tail. He was named Nara-singka Rajan. The queen next gave birth to a daughter. When the children grew up, the parents married them to each other and named them successors to the throne. A lyric poet, who sang exquisitely on the lyre, pleased Nara Singka Rajan so much by his performances, that he was rewarded with an extent of territory, which has since acquired the name of Yalpanam. The Yalpanan reigned with great glory but departed this life without leaving an heir. There was an inter-regnum, during which the country was in a state of commotion. King Seka-rasa-singka Ariyan, son of Seliya Sekaran, with his renowned minister, Puvineya Kayavaku, has come over from Madura at the invitation of Malavan, the son of Selvarayan of Ponpattiyur, the very high caste Vellalan who had come to Jaffna accompanied by the five kinds of dependants. This great king has built the city of Nallur, and entered it in great pomp and ceremony: He bathed, arranged his hair, worshipped the gods duly and applied the sacred ashes. He had on a golden overcoat, a silk cloth, a shawl, a head cloth, ear-rings, rings for the wrists, ankles and fingers, necklaces with pathakkams, a golden waist-string of many folds, a pair of epaulettes and all the other ornaments, especially one on his forehead which was a gift of Malavan. There were the various kinds of instruments of music which sent forth the voice of thunder.

There were the the moon-coloured umbrellas, chowries and torches, the waving of camphor-lights, the sprinkling of perfumes and the hum of Brahmans uttering blessings. The king gave on that day alms of lands. gold, virgins, cows, rice and elephants."

The work next describes the various chiefs and the places assigned to them as in the Vaipavamalai: also the officers appointed by the king.

"One night, as the king lay on his bed, Sivan appeared to him in a dream, and declared himself to be Kayilaya-Nathan, and the king accordingly built a temple". (Its various parts and appurtenances are named.)

The Kethara lingam is sent for, and Kangkathara Aiyar arrives. Then the dedication and the festivities connected with it are described with great minuteness.

## THE ORIGIN OF THE SINGHALESE, TAMIL, MOORISH AND MALAY INHABITANTS OF CEYLON.

The " Singhalese language" is known also by the name of Elu, Helu, Hela-div-bas, Sihela-bas, Sihala-bas and Siya-bas. These are not separate names but are various forms of one and the same word " Elu." Elu becomes Helu, Hela, Sri-hela, Sihela, Sihala, and Singhala. These changes, as every student of oriental literature knows, are neither violent nor uncommon. But " Siya-bas" is somewhat difficult to account for. " Siya" from Siha" is quite natural. The difficulty lies in the absence of the " la" which is in " Sihala." It may be that when the forms Singhala and Sihala had once suggested the " Lion" and the now national story of the " destruction" of the Lion, the destructive portion, supposed to be contained in, but in reality, suggested by, the word " la," gradually passed away from notice and the language became the "Lion's language" (Siyabas), instead of the lion-destroyer's. Likewise the name Ilam, Silam, Seylam, Ceylon, Seyla-dib, Serendib, and Singhaladiv are all adaptations of "Elu" to mean "Elu-land." Now the questions arise " Of what origin is the word " Elu ?" and " What does it mean"? The Elu or Singhalese language (for there is no difference between the two) can return no satisfactory answer to these questions. The common assertion that "Elu" is derived from "Singhala" is based on no scientific principles. The result of the inquiry is that we are driven to ascribe a foreign origin to the term " Elu." That origin can be no other than the Tamil language, and the Vai-pava-malai must be right when it says that the Island bore the Tamil name "Ilam" when Vijayo colonised it and that Vijayo's followers took their name " Singhalese" from the name of the Island.

" Ilam" is a pure Tamil word and has no Ariyan origin. And the Tamil people use it in the following senses and connexions.

Ilam = toddy, gold, Ceylon.

Ila-thesam, Ila-mandalam = Ceylon.

Ilak -kulam, Ilath-thar.<br>Ila-thesath-thar. } = Ceylonese.

Ila-avanam = the Ceylon-avanam, which means 24,000 betel-nuts, as distinguished from Choli-avanam, 20,000 nuts.

Ilath-thalari = the Ceylon species of the flower alari.

Ilath-thuth-thennai = the Ceylon species of the cocoanut palm.

Ilam-suththi-odukirathu= to sail round the Island of Ceylon. In this connexion "Ilam" means the " Island." Casie Chetty (Gazetteer p. 29) says that Ilam is so called from its being "an insular kingdom". But I know of no other authority for saying that Ilam imports the idea of an Island. This Island was named Ilam probably from its mythological origin, being one of the peaks of the golden mountain.

Ilak-katham-pokiravanaip-pol-pesukirathu = to talk like a man who is about to travel the distance of Ceylon i. e. a long journey. This is a proverbial expression, usually said of a timid or lazy man, and had its origin in India. But such is the dominion of words over thought that the Tamils of Ceylon still use the proverb in its original significance.

The geographical situation of Ceylon renders it scarcely conceivable that the Tamils of India could have been ignorant of the existence of the Island before the Vijayan Colonization. Sir William Jones is of opinion that the Island was "beyond time of memory" inhabited by the Hindu race; and he refers to the "languages, letters and old monuments of its various inhabitants" to support it. And Casie Chetty expresses the same opinion (*Gazetteer* p. 51.)

Mr. Clough, the author of the Singhalese dictionary, thinks that Elu was the language of Langka prior to the Singhalese conquest.

Bertolocci (p.p. 12. 18.) and Bennet (p.p. 212. 325), in their accounts of Ceylon, enumerate several facts which tend to shew that the Tamils of India knew and colonized Ceylon long anterior to the Vijayan conquest. The notices of Ceylon contained in the Ramayara and the Mahabharata favour the same view.

The commercial intercourse of the Romans with Ceylon was confined to the northern and western parts of the Island, where the Tamils had a kingdom of their own with Mantotte for its capital. (Journal of the Royal Asiatic Society, Ceylon Branch, 1848, p. 73):—a kingdom which was more ancient than that founded by Vijayo or that by the lutist.

Again neither "Tambapanni," nor "Tammanna" which is derived from "Tambapanni", has anything to do with the story of the palms of the exhausted Magadhis. It is derived from the South Indian River, Tamparaparani, for which the Mahavaliganga was probably mistaken. Or it may be that the early Tamil Colonists brought the name with them.

Parvam Trojam simulataque magnis
Pergama, et arentem Xanthi cognomine rivum
Agnosco. Æneid, III. 349-351.

The Singhalese account of the origin of the names "Singhala" and "Tambapanni" does not seem natural or probable. That account is as follows:—

"At the spot where the 700 men, with the king at the head, exhausted by (sea) sickness and faint from weakness, had landed out of the vessel, supporting themselves on the palms of their hands pressed on the ground, they sat themselves down. Hence to them the name of Tambapanniyo (i. e. copper palmed from the colour of the soil). From this circumstance, that wilderness obtained the name of Tambapanni. From the same cause also, this renowned land became celebrated under that name. By whatever means the monarch

Sihabahu slew the Siho (Lion), from that feat his sons and descendants are called Sihala, (the lion slaying). This Langka having been conquered by a Sihalo, from the circumstance also of its having been colonized by a Sihalo, it obtained the name of Sihala." (Mahawanso, Chap. vii. 47—52).

If this is indeed the true origin of "Singhala," then what is the force of "Hala" in "Saman-hala." As in nature, so in literature, there is a kind of instinct, and, to hold that Srihala and Samanhala have nothing in common, as respects their derivation, would be, to say the least, contrary to that instinct. Samanhala is identical with Selasumano, and the identity will be apparent by simply writing down the intermediate steps. Selasumano = Hela-samano = Samano-hela = Samanhela = Samanhala. Again Helasumano becomes Elasamano, Ilasaman, and Lakshaman. This last form being identical with the name of Rama's brother, it gave rise to the story that Lakshaman was the god of Adam's Peak. The fact is, that Gotama Buddha, whether in India or in Ceylon, was but a mere regenerator, as even the Buddhists must admit, of what had been Samanism before his age. This word, Samanism, is, no doubt, derived from Samano, one of the earliest predecessors of Gotama Buddha, mentioned in the Mahawanso (p. 1.)

The Tamils are a branch of the great Dravida race which inhabit the Dekkan. The Dravidas are supposed to be Scythians of the northern parts of Europe and Asia, who came to India through the northwest passage and settled first between the Himalaya and the Vindia mountains, but were thence gradually driven southwards into the Dekkan by the Ariyans of a prae-ariyan race. That they are Scythians is based upon strong linguistic affinities: but, as respects the other particulars, there is no proof, nor is there even a tradition among the Dravidas to indicate that they had ever occupied northern India. Nevertheless, the religions and literature, the arts and sciences, and the manners and customs of the Dravidas bear ample proof that they have been copied entirely from those of the Ariyans. In fact there is now nothing which the Dravidas can call their own except their dialects. Even their dialects have very largely been modified by the introduction of words and forms from the Sanscrit. To account for the Ariyan elements among the Dravidas, the Ariyan mythology asserts that Agastiya came from the north in the capacity of a missionary to civilize the south. And all Tamil literature acquiesces in this assertion. But no mission of this kind can be sufficient to account for all the phenomena. The matter, however, must rest here, in the absence of more satisfactory information.

The sum of the prae-ariyan civilization of the Dravidas is indeed very small, and Dr. Caldwell states it thus:

"They had 'kings,' who dwelt in 'strong houses,' and ruled over small 'districts' of country! They had 'minstrels' who recited 'songs' at 'festivals' and they seem to have had alphabetical characters' written with a 'style' on palmyra leaves. A bundle of those leaves was called a 'book,'. They were without hereditary 'priests' and 'idols' and appear to have had no idea of 'heaven' or 'hell,' of the 'soul' or 'sin, but they acknowledged the existence of God, whom they styled 'Ko' or King, a realistic title little known to orthodox Hinduism. They erected to his honour a 'temple,' which they called 'Ko-il', God's-house; but I cannot find any trace of the nature of the worship which they offered to him. They had 'laws' and 'customs,' but no lawyers or judges. Marriage existed among them. They were acquainted with the ordinary metals, with the exception of 'tin,' 'lead' and 'zinc'; with the planets which were ordinarily known to the ancients, with the exception of 'Mercury' and 'Saturn'. They had numerals up to a hundred,—some of them to a thousand; but were ignorant of the higher denominations, a 'lakh' and a 'crore'. They had 'medicines,' but no 'medical science,' and no 'doctors'; 'hamlets' and 'towns,' but no 'cities'; 'canoes,' 'boats' and even 'ships' (small 'decked' coasting vessels), but no foreign 'commerce'; no acquaintance with any people beyond sea, except in Ceylon, which was then, perhaps, accessible on foot at low water; and no word expressive of the geographical idea of 'island' or 'continent.' They were well acquainted with 'agriculture', and delighted in 'war'. They were armed with 'bows' and 'arrows,' with 'spears' and 'swords.' All the ordinary or necessary arts of life, including 'spinning,' 'weaving' and 'dyeing' existed amongst them. They excelled in 'pottery', as their places of sepulture show, but were unacquainted with the arts of the higher classes. They had no acquaintance with 'sculpture' or 'architecture'; with 'astronomy'; or even 'astrology'; and were ignorant, not only of every branch of philosophy,' but even of 'grammar' Their undeveloped intellectual condition is especially apparent in words relating to the operations of the mind. Their only words for the 'mind' were the 'diaphragm' (the *phrén* of the early Greeks), and 'the inner parts' or 'interior.' They had a word for 'thought' but no word distinct from this for 'memory,' 'judgment,' or 'conscience'; and no word for 'will.' To express the 'will' they would have been obliged to describe it as 'that which in the inner parts says, I am going to do so and so." (Introduction p.p. 117—118.)

Of the Dravida race, the Tamils are the most important branch. Properly speaking the terms Dravida and Tamil are identical and equipollent. By the operation of certain laws of sound, familiar to all Indian languages, "Dramila,' which is the correct form of the word "Dravida" has become "Tamil." Accordingly, the word "Damilo" is used in the Mahawanso and other Singhalese writings in its most extensive sense, and embraces not merely the Tamil strictly so called, but even the Malayalam, Telugu, Canarese, Tulu, Kudagu, Tuda, Kota, Gond, Ku, Oraon, and Rajmahal, which are all considered as dialects or branches of the Dravida language.

The term Tamil in its restrictive sense, that is, considered as a branch of the Dravida, is applied to the natives of the Chera, Chola and Pandiya Kingdoms.

The Pandiya kingdom once covered the whole extremity of the Indian peninsula and comprehended the greater portion of the Coromandel coast, extending to Canara on the western coast and southwards to the sea. It was subsequently contracted in dimensions by the successive independence of Malabar, the rise of Chera to the west, of Ramnad to the south, of Chola in the east, till it sank in modern times to the petty government of the Naiks of Madura. (Ten. 1. 394). The capital of the Pandiyans was Madura, and their dynasty was supposed to have sprung from the Moon.

The kingdom of Chera was called the Chera Mandalam. It embraced Malayalam or Keralam and extended along the western coast from Cape Comorin to Chandiragiri. Its most northerly place was Palani, the most easterly Trichenkodu, the most westerly Calicut, and on the south, the sea. The Cherans claimed descent from Fire.

The kingdom of Chola was called the Cholomandalam, of which the word Coromandal is a corruption. It embraced Tanjore, Mysore and the districts traversed by the Caveri, and extended from Point Calmiere to the south of the River Krishna. (Casie Chetty's Gazetteer, p.p. 228—229). The Cholans claimed descent from the Sun.

According to Dr. Caldwell, the Tamil language is spoken by 14,500,000 persons. By a census taken in 1871, the number of Tamils in Ceylon, including the Moors, was 705,000, out of a total population in the Island of 2,400,000, of whom 1,670,000, were returned as Singhalese. The distinction between a Tamil and a Singhalese is now a real distinction, and consists in the language, dress, habits and customs of each. But it was not so in early times. "Singhalese" meant an inhabitant of Ceylon, irrespective of race: and the early Singhalese people consisted essentially of Tamils, with a scarcely appreciable admixture of the Magadhi blood. The dress of the Singhalese, their habits, customs and religion were those of the Tamils, and their language, a hybrid of the Tamil and the Magadhi. In support of these assertions, which seem rather bold, a few passages may be cited from the history of Ceylon.

Vijayo, an expatriated prince of (Magadha) Behar, who had sprung from the union of the royal houses of Calingo (the Northern Circars, a Tamil country) and of Bengal (Wango), having been defeated in an attempt to form a settlement in Supparakkapattanam on the coast of Southern India, set sail with 700 followers from the port of Bandar-Maha-Lanka at the mouth of the Godaveri. He was drifting towards Ruhuna, the south-eastern division of this Island, when, having sighted a large rock from the sea, he made for the shore and landed at Periya-thurai near Trincomalie and travelled into the interior of the country, (Rajaratnacari p. 28, Major Forbes II. 79. note.) in accordance with a prediction made at his birth by astrologers that he would go to Sriiake and destroy the devils. (Rajavali p. 167 Ten. I. 330. note).

This happened in the year 543 B.C. Before this period, Ceylon had been inhabited by demons for a space of 1844 years, but there were no human inhabitants in it during that time. (Rajavali p. 168). Vijayo found the Island inhabited not by demons (Yakkhos) only but by Nagas and Dewos also, among whom the Yakkhos held the supreme power.

On their departure from Behar, neither Vijayo nor his followers had been allowed to take with them their women, children or servants. Accordingly they had to form alliances with the natives of the new country. Vijayo set the example and married a Yakkhini, and we may easily imagine that his followers were not slow to copy from him. Aided by their wives, the exiles became masters of a fair portion of the land, and were fathers of a rising progeny of boys and girls, some of whom unfortunately inherited the attributes of the Yakkhos.

Within a few years of their arrival, the Magadhis became firmly settled in the country; but they grew weary of their Yakkho wives, whom they accordingly put away, and, in order to fill their place with more eligible wives, they sent an embassy to the Pandyian, with gems and other presents.

The Pandyian sent out his own maiden daughter with 699 maidens chosen from among his nobility. These 700 ladies landed with their retinue safely at Cottiar. (Cassie Chetty's Gazetteer). The princess was attended by a personal staff of 18 officers of state, 75 menial servants (being horse-keepers, elephant-keepers and charioteers), besides numerous slaves. It may reasonably be assumed that each of these 18 officers was accompanied by his wives and children, his menservants and maid servants and his male slaves and female slaves. In like manner each of the 699 noble maidens was accompanied by attendants, servants and slaves, of both sexes. And there were also numbers of families of each of the five sorts of tradesmen who came to Ceylon on this occasion. (Rajavali p. 175, Tennent. I. 458). These facts swell the number of the original Tamil colonists to at least twenty times that of the Magadhi settlers. And it must be borne in mind that the way once made for these colonists was kept open by a communication which Vijayo carried on with Madura during his whole reign of 38 years. He sent pearls and chanks to his father-in-law from time to time of the annual value of two lakhs. Such a communication could not have failed to lead to a continual influx of the Tamils from the continent in his and the succeeding reigns. On the other hand there was no communication with Behar, and for obvious reasons. The exiles could have hoped to derive no gain or honour from a parent country that had meted out such cruel and degrading punishment, not only upon themselves but even upon their unoffending wives and children. For, we are told in the Mahawanso (chapter VI.) that the people of Magadha desired the instant death of Vijayo and his 700 followers, but that the king put them on board a vessel, and sent them adrift on the ocean, having, nevertheless, previously disgraced them by causing half of their heads to be shaved. In like manner, their wives were disfigured and sent adrift in a second vessel without any males to help them ; and their children too were treated like the women. It is evident that their countrymen designed that they should all perish, and there is but too much reason to suspect that the women and the children did perish. For, although they are said to have landed and settled in Mahindadipo and Naggadipo, yet is there no part of India or Ceylon with which those places have been identified.

A year after the death of Vijayo, however, the Island received a small accession of Magadhi blood. Thirty three male and thirty three female devotees cautiously landed in the Island from Behar. They were devotees in disguise only. One of them was prince Panduvasa, who ascended Vijayo's throne in B.C. 504, another, the princess Baddakkachchana, and the rest were all persons of noble blood. Panduvasa made the princess his queen, and gave the thirty two ladies in marriage to his thirty two companions. Baddakkachchana was soon after joined by six of her brothers from Behar but it does not appear that they brought any families with them. However, on the death of Panduvasa, according to one account, or on that of his son and successor, Abayo, according to another, there was no one, Tamil or Magadhi, to govern the country, which accordingly remained 17 years without a king, until one Gannetissa, probably a native of Ceylon, came to the throne. (Rajaratnacari p. 28 and Knighton p. 14.) After Panduvasa there does not seem to have been any communication between Behar and Ceylon for two centuries.

Under these circumstances it is scarcely probable that the Magadhi settlers, a handful of men, or their descendants, a mixed race, would have invented the name "Singhalese", in order to express a separate origin for themselves, so as to distinguish themselves both from the Magadhis of the continent, and from the pure Tamils of the Island. The term 'Singhalese', according to Singhalese histories, was invented by Vijayo and had a reference to the parentage of his father Sihabahu. The derivation is unmistakably a fanciful one and the whole story of the rape of Suppadevi by a lion is an ingenious invention. The term "Singhalese" does not appear to have been used by or with reference to Sihabahu on the continent: and it could not have been used without a suggestion of shame and degradation, if it really had any connexion with the destruction of the lion.

The existence of such names as Singhababu and Singha Nuwara carries no necessary proof of a leonine parentage, any more than Hastipura and Aswapura prove the existence of races sprung from elephants or horses. Nor can it be supposed that the pure Tamils of Ceylon invented the insulting term and applied it to the mixed race in order to distinguish themselves from that race. True, the pure Tamils were numerically several fold stronger in the Island than the pure and mixed Magadhis, but those Tamils were a people who either came as the dependants of the seven hundred exalted ladies who bestowed themselves upon the Magadhis and became united with those conquerors, or they were mere adventurers who came in the wake of those ladies in order to push their fortune in a new land. They were not therefore likely to have created a distinction that must have been galling to the rulers of the land. The probability is that the pure Magadhis, the pure Tamils and the hybrid offspring, produced, not merely by the mixture of these two races with each other but also, we may presume, with such of the yakkho, nago and dewo tribes as became humanized and joined the new settlers, designated themselves by one common name. That name was "Singhalese." It had no reference to the lion, the lion-killer or the lion-born. It was derived, as the Vaipavamalai derives it and as has been stated elsewhere, from the name by which the Island was known at the time, namely "Singhalam."

The process of coalescence, once happily commenced between the Tamil and Magadhi settlers, continued until it was interrupted by a religious commotion, which took place in B.C. 307, when Buddhism was introduced and established in Ceylon (Tennent I. 339); and the Tamils from the continent who had hitherto been encouraged to become settlers and who, when they arrived, became easily blended with the old settlers, so long as the old settlers followed Saivaism, now changed their character and became invaders. The Buddhist converts (i. e. the old residents) retained their old name, Singhalese, while the new comers and the adherents to the original faith, Saivaism, ranked themselves as Tamils.

The visits of Gotama Buddha to this Island and the assignment of the same date for the landing of Vijayo (B.C. 543) as the death of Gotama must be rejected as "impostures" invented by "sectarian zeal." Mr. William Skeen records it as the result of his investigation among Burmese and other authorities that Buddha never made the visits to Ceylon which the Singhalese ascribe to Buddha. (Journal, Royal Asiatic Society, Ceylon Branch, for 1870-71.) The learned are pretty generally agreed that the age of Gotama has been considerably "post-dated" by Singhalese writers in order to bring about an unnecessary coincidence (Knighton p. 11.) Be this as it may, there is satisfactory evidence that Buddha's religion was not known in the Island till long after the date assigned to the landing of Vijayo. According to the Rajaratnacari, Buddhism was not established till 233 years after the death of Buddha; and all authorities concur in this respect, except the Vaipavamalai which makes Vijayo bring a Buddhist Colony into Ceylon from Siam. The religion of Vijayo and his companions was, even the Vaipavamalai says, Saivaism. And Saivaism continued to be the religion of this Island for no inconsiderable period. Nor did it cease to exist here when it ceased to be the state religion. For, it has continued to exist up to this day. King Raja

Singha I., who ascended the throne in A.D. 1581, was, by religion, a Saivite. He was not a Tamil by birth, but belonged to the ancient dynasty and was the grandson of Wijayabahu VII.

The caste system of the Saivites, with all its ramifications and shades of internal difference, though foreign to Buddhism, has existed in Ceylon in full vigour. There were the high castes, namely, the royal, noble, brahman, chetti, and agricultural: the low castes, namely, the weavers, potters, and such like; and the outcastes, namely, the Chandalas, employed as scavengers and night-men.

The Tamil practices of bali-offering, devil-dancing and the Tamil ceremonies, observed at every step from the conception of the child in its mother's womb to the burning of the dead on the funeral pyre, have maintained their hold up to the present day. Caste distinctions and superstitious ceremonies have such hold on Asiatics that they are observed by even the Christian communities of Ceylon and India. And the whole social and religious fabric of Saivaism as it existed among the Tamils did once flourish in this Island before Buddhism was established in it. If the infant state had commenced with Buddhism for its religion, the existence, at the present day, among the Singhalese, of superstitious practices that are as contrary to pure Buddhism as they are to Christianity, could not be satisfactorily accounted for. (Knighton, p.p. 51, 81, 83, 84, 85.)

Dandris De Silva says, that with the exception of Buddhism (which also is partly, though in some few respects only, based upon Saivaism), every species of superstition, science or literature, which exists among the Singhalese, with certain exceptions of minor importance, may be traced more or less directly to the Vedas and Shastras of the Saivites. (Journal, Royal Asiatic Society, Ceylon Branch, 1865-6). And according to the same authority, demonology was the earliest form of worship in Ceylon, and seven-eighths of the incantations now employed bv the Sinhalese are in the Tamil language.

Dr. Caldwell says "The system which prevails in the forests and mountain fastnesses throughout the Dravidian territories, and also in the south of the peninsula amongst the lower classes and a portion of the middle classes, and which appears to have been still more widely prevalent at an early period, is a system of demonolatry, or the worship of evil spirits by means of bloody sacrifices and frantic dances. This system seems to have been introduced from the Tamil country into Ceylon, where it is now mixed up with Buddhism. On comparing this Dravidian system of demonolatry and sorcery with Shamanism—the superstition which prevails amongst the Ugrian races of Siberia and the hill-tribes on the southwestern frontier of China, which is still mixed up with Buddhism of the Mongols, and which seems to have been the old religion of the whole Tatar race before Buddhism and Mohammedanism were disseminated amongst them—we cannot avoid the conculsion that those two superstitions, though practised by races so widely separated, are not only similar but identical.

The word Shamanism is formed from Shaman, the name of the magician priest of the North Asian demonolaters. Shaman, though a name appropriated by demonolaters, is of Buddhistic origin, and was adopted from the Mongolians. It is identical with Samana, the Tamil name for a Buddhist, and is derived from the Sanskrit word Sramana, a Buddhist ascetic. The use of this word Shaman, in Siberia, must be of comparatively modern origin; but the system of religion into which it has been adopted and incorporated is one of the oldest superstitions in the world.

A full account of the peculiarities of the Dravidian demonolatry was contained in a small work of mine (now out of print), called "The Shânârs of Tinnevelly," published by the Society for the Propagation of the Gospel. I think I proved in that work, that the demonolatry of the Shanars, and other primitive tribes of Southern India, did not originate with the Brahmans, or in any local developement of the religion of the the Brahmans;

but that, on the contrary, the element of demonology which is contained in the Puranic system was borrowed from this old Dravidian superstition. The Buddhists of Ceylon seem to have borrowed their demonolatry from the Dravidians of the old Pandya Kingdom: if so, it cannot be unreasonable to suppose that it was from the same or a similar source that the Brahmans borrowed the demoniacal element contained in their religion. It appears to me that an element of demonism, ready to receive further development, may be traced even in the Aitareya Brahmana of the Rig-veda, in connection with the character attributed and the worship offered, to Rudra, afterwards identified with Siva. I apprehend that we have a mythical record of the adoption of the aboriginal demonolatry into the Brahmanical system, and of the object in view in this alliance, in the Puranic story of the sacrifice of Daksha. According to that story, Siva (*i. e.* Saiva Brahmanism) found himself unable to subdue the old elementary divinities and to secure to himself the exclusive homage at which he aimed, till he called in the aid of the demons (the demonolatry of the aborigines), and put himself at their head in the person of his (pro-re-natus) son, Vira-bhadra; a demi-god, whose wife, emanation, or representative, Bhadra-Kali, is regarded by the Shanars as their patroness and mother." (Comparative Grammar p.p. 580-1).

Vijayo and his immediate successors were, no doubt, Saivites as the Vaipavamalai says. In their eagerness to encourage immigration they tolerated all religions. Sir James Emerson Tennent (Vol. I. pp. 328, 340) says: "Yakkho temples were not only respected but annual demon offerings were provided for them; halls were built for worshippers of Brahma and residences were provided at the public cost for five hundred persons of various foreign religious faiths; but no mention is made in the Mahawanso of a single edifice having been raised for the worshippers of Buddha, whether resident in the Island or arriving among the colonists from India" until the reign of Devanampiya Tisso.

The evidence which the structure of the Singhalese language affords of its affinity to the Dravida languages of the Dekkan, especially Tamil, Telugu and Malayalam, is pronounced by the same authority to be unequivocal. (ib. I. 328.)

The superstitious deference, that had always been paid to Tamil blood, became in later times an article of political faith: and it has prevailed to the latest period of the Singhalese sovereignty, viz., that no individual of pure Singhalese extraction could be elevated to the supreme power. (Casie Chetty's Gazetteer p. 229. Tennent I. 371.) And the quiescence of the Sinhalese to the rule of the Tamils is ascribable, possibly, to the fact that they recognised to some extent the pretensions of the Tamils, as founded on their relationship to the legitimate sovereignty of the Island. (Tennent I. 396.)

On two occasions, princes from the Dravidas were expressly summoned from India when the royal race in Ceylon became extinct. And it will be seen from the following extracts that, from the arrival of Vijayo up to the present time, the Tamils have incessantly migrated into the Island as traders, colonists, conquerors or labourers.

In the reign of Pandukkabhayo, (B. C. 437), Saivaism was the religion of the land, and brahmans were honored for their knowledge of the Vedas and held appointments as purohitos or family priests attached to high caste families.

Buddhism came into Ceylon only in the reign of Deva Nampiya Tisso, (B.C. 307.) It came from the Court of Pataliputto (Patna) and was accompanied by a "royal virgin of great personal charms." The religion and the virgin were both gifts of the Emperor Asoko to King Tisso. The religion was evidently new to the donor and unknown to the donee. Asoko's message to Tisso was couched in these words: "I have taken refuge in Buddha, his religion and his priesthood. I have avowed myself a devotee in the religion of the descendant of Sakya. Ruler of men, imbuing thy mind in the conviction of the truth of these supreme blessings, with unfeigned faith do thou also take refuge in this salvation." (Rajaratnacari p. 33).

In this and several others of his early acts, Asoko betrays all the ardour of a neophyte. But his ardour considerably abated as he grew older. He did not allow his religion to stand between his "carnal passion" and the "charms" of an unbelieving woman:—a woman who did not scruple to raise her impious hand to cut down the sacred bo-tree. (Mahawanso, p. 122.)

The injunction of Mogalli's son, quasi the patriarch of the Buddhists, to the first mission which he sent to "convert" Ceylon and which was headed by Mihindo, a prince of Magadha, was, "Establish, ye in the delightful land of Lanka, the delightful religion of the Vanquisher." On their arrival in Ceylon these missionaries met the king at an elk-hunt and accosted him thus. "Come hither Tisso. We are the ministers and disciples of the lord of the true faith: in compassion towards thee we have repaired hither from Jambudipo." From the circumstance that they styled him simply "Tisso" the king first mistook them for yakkhos. Their first sermons they preached in the "language of the land." But this does not prove that that language, whatever it was, was commonly known in Patna, for, their knowledge of it is evidently supernatural as is proved by the whole career of the mission, as our historians represent it. When the missionaries entered the city, fortune tellers truly prophesied "The land will be usurped by these persons. They will become the lords of this Island." And after this period, the native histories abound with accounts of Buddhist priests and priestesses, sermons and conversions, relics and dagobas, wiharos and bo-trees, and presents to priests and gifts to temples. Still there was no communication with Behar.

Tisso died in B.C. 267, and within 30 years of his death, *i. e.*, in the reign of Suratissa (B.C., 237), the religious convulsion of which he was the author was, as may be expected. followed by a political one. Two Tamil or Saivite princes, Sena and Gutika who were in the service of the king, rose against their master, put him to death, restored Saivaism and reigned from Anuradhapura. (Knighton p. 29.) After a reign of 22 years. they were overthrown and put to death by Aselo or Ayelo a descendant of the old dynasty. (Rajavali p. 187. Mahawanso p. 127)

When Aselo had reigned ten years, the kingdom was usurped again, in B. C. 205, by a new Tamil, Elaro or Ellala, of the Uju tribe, who came from Chola with a following of 1,080,000 armed Tamils, assumed the reins of government over the whole Island, raised 32 bulwarks and built many cities (Rajavali p. 187). Elaro was a Saivite, and, though he despised Buddhism he administered justice with impartiality to "friends" and "foes", and protected the Buddhist priests. He was so just that the elements obeyed him, and so magnanimous that he disdained to make an attack without "giving the enemy full intimation of his intention." (Knighton p. 35.) At this period, the three geographical divisions of the Island, made during the reign of Panduvasu, became three separate kingdoms. The chief and most powerful of them was the Pihiti or Rajaratta, which was under the Tamils. It consisted of all the country lying to the north of the Mahaweliganga and Dedru Oya. Ruhuna, the second, was under the Singhalese but paid tribute to the Tamils (Rajavali p. 188. Tennent, I. p. 395). It consisted of all the south-eastern portion of the Island lying between the Kaluganga and the Mahawaliganga. Its capital was Mahagam and its king was Kakawanno, father of Dutugamini (Mahawanso, pp. 130, 162.) It was so continually exposed to the inroads of the Tamils that the king kept his son Dighabayo posted at the Kachchakkathiththiya and Prince Gamini's son, Tisso, at Dighawapi in Batticaloa. (Mahawanso p.p. 138. 144). The third, Maya. was under Deva Nampiva Tisso's brother, Uttiyo or Yatalattisso, who built the Calany temple. It lay between the mountains, the two great rivers and the sea, having the Dedru Oya to the north and the

Kaluganga as its southern limit, (Rajaratnacari p. 37. Tennent I. p. 337.) In the centre of the Island and bounded by these three divisions there was the Malaya country usually reckoned as part of Maya, but it was generally independent of the three kingdoms.

After a reign of 44 years, Ellala was slain in battle, in B. C. 161, by the famous Dutugamini, who put to death, if the Rajaratnacari (p. 38) is to be trusted, eight million Tamils on the occasion. But the Rajavali (p. 221) gives 1,080,000 as the number of Tamils slain throughout the whole war between Gamini and Ellala.

Seven days after Ellala's death, his nephew, Ballukkho, landed at Mantotte with an army of 30,000 Tamils from the continent, and shared the fate of his uncle. (Rajavali p. 219.)

This King Dutugamini had in his youth undergone the ceremony of ear piercing and wore ear ornaments throughout his life. Wearing ear-rings is purely a Tamil practice but it was once general among the Singhalese. In later days, (i. e. about A.D. 38) it became the distinguishing mark of a particular caste, the lambakhannos. (Mahawanso p.p. 135, 156, 216, 228.) The Veddhas bored the ears of their children and decorated them with rings (Tennent II. p. 443.)

Dutugamini was the first Ceylonese monarch who openly and mainly relied on the religious differences between himself and the enemy as a means to rouse the enthusiasm of his soldiers, or quiet his own disturbed conscience. Before marching against Elaro he declared his object to be "the restoration of the religion" and proclaimed "I fight not for dominion but for the sake of the religion of Buddha." When he was tormented with remorse for the countless lives he had destroyed, he was consoled by the assurance of the priesthood that "heretics are sinners and on par with wild beasts. As thou wilt cause the religion of Buddha to shine forth in great splendour, on that account, O ruler of men subdue thy mental affliction."

And this ruler of men subdued his mental affliction and "extirpated the religion imported into Ceylon by his enemies." (Mahawanso p. 158. Rajavali p. 222) Notwithstanding the extirpation of Hinduism, the prejudices of caste were so great at this period that Sali the son of Dutugamini forfeited his crown by his marriage with a low-caste maid. And about two hundred years after this, (namely in A. D. 38.), we shall find King Ilanaga losing his kingdom in a rebellion which was caused by his appointing one of an inferior caste as the judge of a superior. (Knighton pp. 41, 92). In law, up to a very recent period, caste was an important ingredient in determining questions of adoption and matrimony.

In B. C. 103, seven Tamil chiefs from Chola landed at Mahatirta (Mantotte) with seven armies, and, being joined by a Saivite prince of Nakula in Ruhuna, drove the reigning King Walagambahu I. into concealment among the mountains near Adam's Peak, sent away his queen as captive to the coast of India with the Bonapatraya (Buddha's cup), conquered the northern parts of the country and reigned 14½ years.

But in the year B. C. 88, Walagambahu overcame the Tamils and recovered his capital. He was a great supporter of Buddhism and destroyed Saivite temples : he caused 500 priests to assemble at Aluvihara near Matale and reduced into writing the doctrines and discourses of Buddha which had been orally delivered by Mahindo and previously preserved by tradition alone. Those writings are called the Pitakataya; and their commentaries, the Athakatha. (Tennent I. p. 376, Rajaratnacari, p. 43).

But his grandson and successor, Chora Naga, was a Saivite and destroyed Buddhist temples. (Mahawanso p.p. 202-207, Knighton, p.p. 44,47. Rajavali p. p. 223, 224, 226.) And his queen, the infamous Anula, who ascended the throne in B. C 47 and reigned 5 years, raised to her bed and throne among her numerous other lovers, two Tamils, one a carpenter and the other a purohita Brahman. (Mahawanso p.p. 208-209.)

In A. D. 42, Ellona or Elanna, a deposed king of Ceylon, returned from the continent with a foreign army which had been mainly levied from among the Tamils, and by means of it he regained his ancient throne. (Knighton p. 92, Rajaratnacari pp. 53, 54.)

In A. D. 110, during the reign of Wankanasiko Raja, the Tamils of Chola invaded Ceylon and not only carried away twelve thousand Ceylonese families as slaves to Mysore but exacted an annual tribute of slaves. Within 3 years, however, not only were the Singhalese captives recovered by Gajabahu I., who invaded the Chola Rata, but he in turn brought 12,000 Tamil families as captives from the banks of the Kaveri and established them at Alutkur Corle. He recovered also the Bonapatraya. (Knighton pp. 94, 95, Rajaratnacari pp. 57, 58. Rajavali p. 231.)

In A. D. 209 Abhayo, a brother of the reigning king, Wairatissa brought an army of Tamils from the continent, and having defeated the king, became at once the master of the Island, and, as might be expected, the slave of his own army. The Waytoolian heresy, which was but a mere introduction of Saivite rites into Buddhism and which arose in the preceding reign, broke out afresh in this reign and was supported by the Saivite army. The King was too powerless to put it down effectually, notwithstanding his efforts at repression. He only succeeded in exiling a few of its priests, who however found a refuge from persecution amongst their sympathizers in the Dekkan. (Tennent 1. p. 380, Knighton p. 96.)

In the reign of Golu Abha (A. D. 248-261), the Waytoolian heresy was revived and it was embraced by the Abhayagiri priests, many of whom were in consequence banished. (Knighton p. 98.)

King Maha Sen, the last of the Great dynasty, who reigned between A. D. 275 and 302 according to Turnour, or between 271 and 298 according to Knighton (p. 350), was a pupil of a Waytoolian priest, Sangha-mittra, and at first persecuted the Buddhists, demolished 364 of their sacred edifices and encouraged the Hindus, but he afterwards repented and demolished the dewalays in the Saivite villages and built wiharos in their place. (Rajavali p. 167, Knighton p. 99). The kings who followed Maha Sen were of the mixed blood, sprung from the union of the Suriya race with that of the bringer of the bo-tree or with that of the Saivite prince and princess of Calinga who brought the Dalada to Ceylon. (Rajavali p. 239, Knighton p. 100.)

King Soothi Sena and his sister who deposed him (A. D. 428) were children of King Mahanamo by a Tamil consort. (Knighton p. 102.)

In the reign of Mitta Sena, who ascended the throne in A. D. 433, Pandu, a Tamil, and four others of his countrymen landed in Ceylon with a large army, took the capital and established their sway and religion over Ceylon. (Mahawanso, Note p. 100. Rajaratnacari p. 75. Rajavali, p. 243.) But the Tamil reign lasted only 27 years. (Rajavali p. 243.) For, Dhatu Sena or Dhasenkeliya destroyed both the government and the religion of the Tamils (A. D. 459); and, the Mahawanso adds, that he also extirpated the Tamils. This statement ought to be received with due allowance for the national vanity and family partiality of its author, Maha Namo, who was uncle of Dhatu Sena and lived in his reign. There is no doubt however that Dhatu Sena oppressed the Tamils: for it is said that he degraded the Sinhalese who had intermarried with the Tamils, and that he confiscated their estates. He organised a naval force to keep all invaders out of the Island. (Tennent I. 390. 398, 399.)

In A. D. 495, the second son of King Dhatu Sena, Mogallano, who led a wandering life in India, returned with a powerful army and overcame his brother, the parricide Kasyappa, the reigning king of Ceylon. (Knighton p. 105, Rajavali p. 244.) Mogallano also established a marine force to guard the Island against the descents of the Tamils. (Tennent I. 393.)

In A. D. 534, there was a religious persecution in which the Saivites were "extirpated" and their books burnt. This was the third persecution of the Saivites (Knighton p. 107), and after it, there was a cessation of their incursions for a period of a hundred years, at the end of which, it was renewed with redoubled vigour and kept up for four hundred years.

During this period of four hundred years the Tamils filled every office in the land and raised and dethroned kings at will. (Tennent I. p. 399). One of the kings of Chola, Vera-devan, reckoned Ceylon among his possessions.

In A. D. 633, there was a civil war in Ruhuna, which resulted in the defeat and capture of the Tamil mercenaries who had come in the previous reigns. The captives were distributed as slaves to the temples. (Knighton p. 109, Tennant I. p. 400.)

In A.D 649, Srisangaboo II., who had been driven from this kingdom, returned with a powerful army of Tamils from the continent. This army was shortly reinforced by another from the same place, and by the united exertion of the two, he was reinstated on his ancient throne. He was again driven from the throne and he again recovered it by the aid of a Tamil army. (Knighton, p.p 109-110. Rajavali. p. 247.)

In A.D. 693, Dalupiatisso II, who had been a refugee on the continent, having been invited by the resident Tamils of Ceylon. whom the reigning King, Dapulu II, had in vain attempted to drive away from the capital, returned with an army of Tamils and recovered his patrimony. (Knighton p. 110.)

In A. D. 702, Srisangaboo III, set up a figure of the god Vishnu for the use of his Tamil subjects, though he himself was a follower of Buddhu.

In A. D. 720, Mahalaipamu. a scion of the royal blood of Ceylon, who was in the military service of the King of Magadha, of which country, by the way, nothing had been heard of in Ceylon for many centuries, came with a large army probably raised in Magadha, and after suffering severe reverses, put the reigning king, Hathadatha, to death and ascended the throne of Ceylon. (Knighton p. 111.)

In A. D. 769, the seat of government was removed by Aggrabodhi IV from Anurajapura to Pollannaruva with the avowed object of avoiding the proximity of the Tamils, who were become masters of all the north. (Knighton, p. 112.)

According to the Rajaratnacari (p.p. 81-82), the removal of the seat of government to Pollannaruva took place in A.D. 819, and in the reign of the Saivite king Matwalasseu.

In A. D. 840, the Tamils of Pandi over-ran the north of Ceylon, reduced the whole Island to the position of a tributary and returned to their country, carrying away spoils of great value.

But in A. D. 858, Casiapu IV. lent aid to one of the sons of the king of Pandi who had revolted against his father. Casiapu crossed the sea in person, reached the seat of war with a large army composed chiefly of Tamils, over-ran the Dekkan, plundered Madura, placed the rebel son on the throne of his father, and returned home laden with spoils. (Knighton p.p. 122, 130, Tennent I, 401).

In the reign of Casiapu VI., A. D. 954, assistance was again sent from Ceylon to the Pandiyan under the leadership of Sekka Sen, the king's son, in a quarrel which the Pandiyan had with his neighbour the Cholan. The Pandiyan was, after a long struggle, defeated and had to take refuge in Ceylon, whence he was afterwards expelled for conspiring against his benefactor, Dapulo VI., in A. D. 964. (Tennent I. 592, Knighton p. 125.)

The reign of Udaya IV. (A. D. 990,) was disturbed by an invasion of the Island by the Tamils of Chola, which was at first successful but was afterwards repulsed with the aid of the mountaineers of Ruhuna. (Knighton p. 127).

In A. D. 997, Mibindo III. who repaired the edifices at Adam's Peak which the Chola Tamils had destroyed, obtained a queen from Calinga, (Knighton p. 127).

In the reign of Mihindo's son and successor, Sena IV., (A. D. 1013,) when there was a civil war, the Tamil residents in the country united together and fought for the royal family against the Singhalese insurgents and restored i to power. (Knighton p. 127-128).

In the reign of Mihindo IV., A. D. 1023, who retransferred the seat o government from Pollannaruva to Anarajapura, the Choleans invaded Ceylon captured the royal family, and having sent it captive to Chola, established a Tamil Viceroy at Pollannaruva, and held uninterrupted possession of the Island for thirty years. (Knighton p. 128, 129, 130, Tennent I. 402).

Speaking of these troublous times the Rajaratnacari says that the Tamils kept up a continual war with the Ceylonese for 250 years, coming down frequently in large numbers, amounting to near a lakh at a time; they filled every city and village in the Island and abolished the religion of Buddha (Rajaratnacari p. 85). And throughout the reign of 19 kings, extending over 86 years from A. D. 965 to 1071, the Tamils were supreme and they extirpated the priests of Buddha. (Rajavali p.p. 251-252.)

In A. D. 1025, when Mahmood of Ghuzni over-threw the temple of Somnath, the terrified Hindus betook themselves to Ceylon and settled in various parts of it. (Tennent I. 561.)

Wijayabahu who came to the throne in A. D. 1071, received an aid, from Siam, of treasure, made war on the Tamils and after repeated reverses, drove them to their own country. But such had been the tyranny of the Tamils that scarcely a high priest of note was found in the Island, and high priests had to be sent for from Aramana (Rangoon) in the Siamese Peninsula. (Knighton p.p. 130—132).

King Parakkramabahu, A. D. 1153 to 1186, first reduced Ruhuna under his power, and in the 16th year of his reign sent out an expedition against Cambodia and Rangoon for the purpose of avenging the insults which the inhabitants of those places had offered to him, by plundering elephant merchants of Ceylon and by intercepting and carrying away some of the princesses of his household, whom he had sent on a voyage to the continent. This expedition consisted of 2,125,000 picked men and was commanded by a Tamil Athikaram. It inflicted severe losses on the enemy and obtained full satisfaction. He sent out another expedition, which was commanded by his minister Lankanathan, and directed against Kulasekara Cholan who had taken Parakkirama Pandiyan prisoner, reduced his kingdom to the position of an apanage of Chola and placed over it Sundara Pandiyan, a son of Parakkirama Pandiyan. This expedition joined Virapandiyan, another son of Parakkirama Pandiyan, and reduced Ramesaram and six neighbouring provinces, defeated king Kulasekara Cholan, who had now assumed the name of Kulasekara Chola Pandiyan, drove his feudatory, Sundara Pandiyan, from Madura and placed Virapandiyan on the throne. The king of Chola made three attempts to reoccupy Madura, but being successively defeated, surrendered himself and made the required concessions. Accordingly Arravana (Coramandel) also became a tributary of Ceylon. (Rajavali p. 254, Rhys Davids, Journal of the Asiatic Society of Bengal, No. 2, 1872, cited by Dr. Caldwell in his Comp. Gram., p. 538, Knighton p. 144.)

In conformity with the tolerant spirit of Buddhism, this king erected a house for the Saivites of Ceylon for the worship of their own gods. (Tennent I, 407 )

Kirte Nissanga, who commenced his reign in A. D. 1187 and reigned nine years, was not of the royal family of Ceylon but of Calinga. And queen Kaliyanawati (who reigned six years from A. D. 1202) was his sister. (Knighton 148.)

In the reign of Dharmasoko, A. D. 1208, Manikunga or Dinunam, a Tamil from Chola, conquered Ceylon by means of a large army of his countrymen, whom he brought with him, but was slain after a reign of 17 days at Pololnuvara. (Knighton, p. 151. Rajavali, p. 255.)

Another Tamil, Lokaiswara appeared within a year and was at first successful but was defeated in battle and deposed after a short reign of nine months. A third Tamil, Parakkiramapandiyan, appeared in A. D. 1211. He conquered the Island, but only reigned three years, when a fourth Tamil, Magha, who came from Calinga with an army of 24,000 Tamils and 1,000 Malays, took the city of Colon Nuwara and became king of the whole Island. He reduced the hitherto independent Ruhuna and established a stronghold at Mahagam: and, thence to Jaffnapatam every part of the Island was under his sway. (Tennent I. pp. 412-413. Knighton p. 451.)

During his long reign of 20 years, the Tamils destroyed dagobas, desecrated monasteries, propagated Saivaism, dishonoured virgins and women of rank, reduced the most dignified by birth and rank to the position of menials, and thus they governed and kept all in subjection. (Rajaratnacari p. 93. Knighton pp. 152, 153. Rajavali, p. 256, 257.)

But Wijayababu III, who had concealed himself in Maya, recovered a portion of his kingdom from Magha (A. D. 1235), built the city of Dambadenia or Jambudrona, 50 miles to the north of the present Colombo, in Maya. He reigned 24 years and re-instated Buddhism within his dominion. (Knighton p. 153). The Rajavali (p 257), says that he united all the three parts of the kingdom under his own government, but Pihiti continued to remain as before under the Tamils, who had a line of forts from Uratotte on the west through Pollannaruva to the east, which they had filled with 40,000 soldiers. (Rajavali p.p. 258, 260. Rajaratnacari p. 94). To escape the proximity of the Tamils, he removed the seat of government from Pollannaruva to Dambadenia

Kalikala or Pandita Parakkramabahu II, who came to the throne in A.D 1267, "annihilated all the power which had been acquired by the Tamils during the reign of the preceding 12 kings." (Rajaratnacri p. 95, Rajavali p. 258) But he had to encounter a new race of marauders, the Malays.

The Malays made a descent on the Island in A.D. 1278, under their leader Chundrachano or Chandrabahu, a Tamil king, but were utterly defeated. They made a second descent and were now assisted by the Pandiyan and the Cholan but were again defeated. (Knighton p. 157, Rajavali, p. 260.)

But to escape the Tamil invasions for the future, the king built (in A.D. 1287) Sriwardanapura in the mountains of Maya in the seven korles, which afterwards (A.D. 1271) became the capital under the name of Sengkadagala Neuwara or Kandi. This reign is remarkable for two literary events. Dharmakirti continued the Mahawanso from the reign of Mahasen, and Mairupade compiled the Poojawaliya. (Knighton p.p. 156-158.)

Throughout the whole of this reign, which lasted 40 years, the king made war against the Tamils, built 15 forts in order to keep them out, and fought 12 pitched battles against their king Tambalingama. (Rajaratnacari p.p. 100-104.) At his death, his power extended over the 250,000 villages of Maya, 450,000 of Pihite, and 770,000 of Ruhuna. (Rajavali p.p. 262-263.)

In the reign of Bosat Wijayabahu IV (A.D. 1301-1303), a Tamil, Maha Desa Raja, with an army of the nation, called Siganam, landed in Ceylon and carried away the king and many of his subjects as prisoners to his country Maha China. (Rajavali p. 263.)

After this there was no king in Ceylon. The minister, Allakaiswara was in Rygam Nuwara, and a son-in-law of Parakkramabahu remained in Sampala Nuwara. Both these paid tribute to Aryachchakkra-varthi, King of the Ceylonese Tamils, who reigned from Jaffnapatam (Rajavali p 264.) But according to Rajaratnacari (p. 107), Wijayabahu had a successor, king Buvenekabahu I. of Yapahu, whose reign extended between A.D. 1303 and 1314, and who was "monarch of the three kingdoms of Ceylon." According to Knighton, (p. 161) on the death of Buveneko (A.D. 1314), Ariya Chakkravarthi came from the Coromandel Coast with a large army, laid the country waste, extirpated the religion of Buddha and sent the Dalada as a spoil to the king of the Carnatic named Kula Sekara Raja of Pandi who had sent Ariya Chakkravarthi to Ceylon. (Rajavali p. 108, Knighton p. 161).

On Ariya Chakkravarthi's departure, Parakkramabahu III (A.D. 1314-1319) was raised to the throne, and he recovered the Daladá by submission and tribute. (Rajaratnacari p. 108). But he removed the capital from Yapahu to Hastisailapura or Kurnegalle for fear of the Tamils. For the same reason Gampola was chosen in A. D. 1347.

King Wikkrama Bahu III. (A. D. 1371-1378), or more properly his minister Alakaiswara, who built Cotta "conquered all the Tamils who occupied the 18 pattoos of the Vanni, and thus remained king of 256,000 villages in the province of Matara, 495,000, in the province of Jaffna, 790,000 in the province of Uva" as sole monarch of the whole Island. (Knighton p. 163, Rajaratnacari p. 112.)

But Ceylon was again invaded by Ariya Chakkrawarthi, who had formerly carried off the Dalada in 1314, and who now threw up fortifications in Colontotta, Negombo and Chilaw, reduced the northern division of the Island into entire subjection and fixed the seat of his government at Jaffnapatam. Besides governing the northern kingdom, Aryan reduced Alakaiswara to the necessity of paying an annual tribute. But Alakaiswara soon shook off this yoke. (Rajavali p. 265, Knighton p. 163.)

Wijayabahu VI. who ascended the throne in A. D. 1398 expelled several gangs of the Tamils who were roaming through the country in search of pillage. (Knighton p. 164.)

And his successor Parakkramabahu VI. (A. D. 1410-1462) who removed the seat of government to Cotta sent his son Sapoomal Kumara against the Tamils of the northern part of the Island and reduced them to complete subjection. The prince entered the city of Jaffna and made such carnage in the midst of the Tamils that the streets of Jaffna ran with blood that day as if it had been a river. The king Arya Chakkrawarthi who was a successor of the original conqueror of the same name, fell into the prince's hands and was put to death. His wife and children were brought to Cottah and presented to Parakkramabahu, (Rajavali p. 269 and Kovulsandese.) Jaffna was reduced to a province and its government was conferred on Sapoomal Kumara who went thither to rule it in person. The king carried on a commerce with his son's territories, but one of his vessels laden with goods was seized by Wirarama a Malay, who belonged to Jaffna. The king sent a flotilla which took Wirarama and put him to death. The flotilla then made a descent on Chola and reduced four towns of the place called Makudamkottah to the necessity of paying tribute to the king of Ceylon. The king's second son Ambulugala Cumara reduced the kings of Kandi and Gampola. (Rajavali p.p. 268-270).

In the reign of Dharmaparakkramabahu IX. (A. D. 1505-1527), a great number of Moors—a race who are believed to have made their first appearance in Ceylon about the 8th century, (Knighton p. 157)—led by a chief called Caderwawa from Cayilpatnam made a landing at Chilaw but were opposed and defeated. They lost their Captain in the engagement, and 89 of their number were taken prisoners and brought to Cottah. (Rajavali p. 274).

But the most important event in the history of Ceylon took place in this reign. It was the landing of the Portuguese in A. D. 1505. Francisco De Almeyda, whom they sent over unknown seas in search of the Moors, their enemies in the carrying trade, was driven by a current to Galle, and soon after, they built a fortress at Colombo. In 1517 the Moors laid siege to it but their efforts proving ineffectual, they renewed their attack in 1520, but were again unsuccessful. (Tennant II. p.p. 9, 10.)

In the reign of the Emperor Buweneka VII. of Cottah, (1534-1542), his brother Mayadunnai a tributary king who ruled over Sitawake raised a rebellion, and seized Raygam Corle, (Ribeyro p. 25), because the Emperor entertained an idea of leaving the kingdom to his grandson Periya Bandara or Don Juan Dharmapala, the offspring of his daughter Samudra Devi by her husband Vijayabandara, son of the daughter of the king of Madampe by a Tamil nobleman from Chola. (Rajavali p. 286.)

The rebel king courted the alliance of the Samorin of Calicut and other Tamils and brought a great number of people belonging to the tribe of Wadak Caros from Colilak and with the assistance of the Moorish chiefs Cudely and Paichi Marikkar invaded Cottah. But the Wadak Caroos were totally defeated, not being able to stand against the fire of the Portuguese who fought on the side of the Emperor (Rajavali p.p. 288-290, Ribeyro, p. 25).

After Samudra-devi's death, Vijaybandara married a daughter of Mayadunnai and thereupon peace was made between the brothers. But a number of years afterwards, having obtained an auxiliary force from the continent, headed by a follower of Mahomet, Maya Dunnai sought a quarrel with Buvenekabahu. Buvenekabahu marched out with a Singhalese army, taking the Portuguese to his assistance as before. He was eminently successful, and Maya Dunnai purchased peace by a treacherous surrender of the chiefs of his Moorish allies. In the following year, the Emperor was accidentally slain at Calany by a shot from the musket of a Portuguese. (Rajavali p. 289-290.)

He was succeeded by Dharmapala in A. D. 1542, who afterwards embraced the Christian religion and was baptized by the name of Don Juan. His example was followed by many of the nobles. "And from this day the women of the principal people of Cotta, also those of the lower castes, for the sake of Portuguese gold, began to turn Christians and live with the Portuguese. And the priests of Buddha repaired to Sitawak and Kandi." (Rajavali 291.)

Don Juvan defeated Maya Dunnai, pursued him to Sitawak and thence drove him to Daraenigala. But his own father and Maydunnai's son-in-law, Vijaya, was taken by stratagem and put in prison, and Vijaya's brother Tammitta was sent to Goa. "Such" says the native historian "are the results of Buvenekabahu's folly in admitting the Portuguese: he was himself killed, his adopted son was caused to change his religion, Vijaya was cast in prison, Tammitta was transported to Goa, high caste women mixing with men of low castes, the high among the people have been degraded, and the low castes have been exalted. Thus did Buvenekabahu a great deal of mischief to that religion which must endure for so long a time." (Rajavali p. 292-293.)

Vijaya, however, soon escaped from prison and after several vain attempts to found a new kingdom, repaired to Jaffnapatam with his son Vijeya Pala, (Rajavali p. 293), in the hope of enlisting the Tamils into his service, but while remaining in Tharakkuli, the father and son were killed by the Tamils for the sake of their wealth. (Rajavali 301.)

Maya Dunnai's son, Raja Singha I. made himself independent and reigned as Emperor from Sitawak, (A. D. 1581-1592), while Don Juvan Dharma Pala was in the fort of the Portuguese. Raja Singha defeated Jaiweera king of Sengkadagala Nuwara (Kandi) and pursued him through Dumbara pattoo until he took refuge in the jungle near Jaffna. (Tennent II. p.p. 17-21.) But Dharma Pala went to his assistance at the head of an army consisting of Portuguese and Singhalese soldiers. He set sail from Colombo, disembarked at Mannar, went to Jaffna and brought away the king and his court, his queen and his daughter. On their way the Raja and his queen died, and the court and princess remained at Mannar. (Rajavali p 307.)

This Raja Singha though a grandson of Wijeyabahu VII., was by religion not a Buddhist but a Saivite. He cherished an implacable hatred to Buddhism, which he extended to Christianity also. He had a mohattiar in his employ, of the name Aree Juvan Wenda Perumal or Manampairy, a Tamil who came from Chola as a pilgrim. This mohottiar married a daughter of Raja Chetti, who had been the king's concubine and became a great favourite of the king. He fought many battles against the Portuguese and defeated Juda Sulva Modliar, a valiant Moorish captain whom the Portuguese had sent against him. (Rajavali p. 312-316.)

Raja Singha died in A. D. 1592, at the advanced age of 120 and was succeeded by Raja Sooria Cumara. This prince lost his life by a conspiracy raised against him by his subjects, because he cohabited with a low caste woman. (Rajavali p. 314.)

Don John Wimala Dharma, a scion of the original royal family, became Emperor and reigned from Kandi (A. D. 1592-1604.) He favoured Buddhism and restored its forgotten rites, not however from a conviction of its truth, but from a hatred of Christianity. (Tennent II. 22.)

In 1602 the Dutch landed in Batticaloa and obtained permission to build the fort of Cottiar. Immediately on its erection (A. D. 1612) it was surprised and destroyed by the Portuguese. (Tennent II. p.p. 36-38.)

The first attempts of the Portuguese to reduce Jaffna were made in 1544, but the king of Jaffna purchased peace by agreeing to pay 4,000 ducats yearly. (Tennent II. 28.) In the same year such numbers embraced Christianity in Mannar that 600 of the converts were put to death by the king. The Portuguese made war upon him, and took his city in 1864, but restored it to him on his agreeing to pay £11,000 and disclose certain treasures supposed to be hiden in his territories. (Ten II. 29.)

In 1591 and 1604, fresh troops were sent to punish him for assisting the Singhalese in their opposition to the Portuguese. But on each occasion the king readily submitted. But in 1617, an expedition was directed against Jaffna, and it captured the city with circumstances of singular barbarity, and extinguished the Tamil dynasty. The king was carried captive to Goa and there executed. (Tennent II. 31.)

In 1622, the Tamils of India made an attempt to recover Jaffna and sent an army thither but failed. (Tennent II. p. 31.)

In the reign of Raja Singha II. of Kandi, (A. D. 1635-1685), against whom the Portuguese led an army of 28,000 Tamils and 700 Europeans, the Portuguse were ignominiously defeated. This king was an atheist and an infidel and rejected the Ordinances of Buddhism.

In A. D. 1658, the Dutch took Mannar, and marching thence through the country of the Vanni, invested the fort of Jaffnapatam, which capitulated on terms. (Tennent II. p. 46.)

Wimala Dharma II., (A. D. 1685-1707) restored Buddhism to its original splendour. He sent an embassy to Siam and procured 12 upasampada or chief priests. (Tennent II. p. 61.)

Passing over the reign of Kundisala, (A. D. 1707-1739), with whom the royal Sinhalese line became extinct, and that of the Tamil Prince, Sri Wijeya Singha Raja, (A. D. 1739-1747), we come to the reign of Kirti Sri Singha (A. D. 1781.) whose chief care was to purify and reform the religion of the state. He obtained priests and ministers from Siam and once more Buddhism lifted its venerable head above the trammels of infidelity.

The Portuguese, whose period extended between A. D. 1505 and 1640, were under a sentiment of religious bigotry, and they did not neglect their opportunities for propagating their faith, but the Dutch, (1640-1796), who were not less jealous, refused to allow any but Christian natives to hold situations under them.

In 1796, when the English appeared before Colombo, its cowardly occupants sent a body of Malays headed by a Frenchman against the invaders. The Frenchman fell and the Malays retreated with precipitation.

In the following year, Tamil Dubashes were placed by the English in situations formerly occupied by the Ceylonese. This measure caused numerous revolts, which immediately ceased on the restoration of the native officers.

On the death of Rajadhi Raja Singha of Kandi, in A. D. 1798 Pilma Talava raised a Tamil youth of inferior rank to the throne, with the name of Sri Wickrama Raja Singha. The late king's queen and her brother, Mutusamy, fled to the English and were protected at Jaffna.

In 1803, there was a company of Malays in the army of Major Davie and was commanded by the famous captain Nouradien, whom the offers of life, service, honours and command could not induce to desert the English standard.

In A. D. 1815, when Sri Wickrama Raja Singha was captured, he had an escort of Tamils, who defended him strenuously but were finally overcome.

The above is a brief and a necessarily imperfect account of the arrivals of the various colonists of Ceylon, and the part they have played in its history. Imperfect as it is, it is impossible to rise from its perusal without being impressed with the conviction that the Tamil element is by far the most predominant in the colonization of Ceylon.

The Singhalese race sprang from a mixture the Magadhi and Tamil blood in the proportion of one Magadhi to twenty Tamil, and this mixed race has been receiving and absorbing into itself, for a period of 2,400 years, a continual stream of fresh Tamil blood, to the almost entire exclusion of the Magadhi. So that in an ethnological point of view the Singhalese are but a branch of the Tamil race. How far there may be philological or other reasons to lead to a different conclusion, it is not our province to investigate here. This essay was undertaken only to account for the presence in Ceylon, of the Tamils, the Moors and the Malays, by the side of the Singhalese and the part they have had in its political history. But it has led to an unexpected, and nevertheless, a most gratifying result.

The feelings with which the Singhalese, the Tamils, the Moors, and the Malays have regarded each other have been different at different times. But under the British rule they are living in uniform peace and amity.

## THE MOORS.

The Moors are (by race) pure Tamils of Southern India who have been converted to Islamism. Although the term " Moor", which is the same as " Maur", means a " Mauritanian, i. e., an inhabitant of Morocco in Africa, yet it does not prove an African origin for the race, for, the term " Moor" was applied, at one time, even in Europe, to describe all Mahommadans, irrespective of the country of their origin. Accordingly, the Tamil form Maurikkar, (derived from Morocco), means, in Ceylon, nothing more than " Mahommadans." The same remark applies to the " Tulukkar" i.e. " Turks", a name by which the Mahommadans are generally spoken of in India, and occasionally in Ceylon. The principal seat of the Moors in India was Kayilpatanam, and thence they have spread as far as Ramesvaram and Ceylon. The Singhalese call them, " Marakkalayas" which is but a corruption of the Tamil " Maurikkayar", and has nothing to do with boatmen as Casie Chetty supposes. The Tamils call them, " Sonakar" a name by which they are also known among themselves. Father Beschi in his Tamil Dictionary explains the term, " Sonakar" to be a corruption, meaning Chola-nakara-people. But its true origin is, "Suni" or " Soni" one of the two great rival sects among the Mahommadans. In Batticaloa and some other parts of the Island the term "Soni" is frequently applied to a Moor, instead of the honorific term, Sonakar. The word " Sonakar" occurs in the Tamil Ramayanam, Book I. Chap 11. Stanza 99. It is found there in company with the " Vedar" and " Chinar." The Tamil Ramayanam was composed according to a stanza in it, in the Saka year 807, but, according to Dr. Caldwell, in the reign of Rajendra Chola, who commenced to reign in A. D. 1066 and ruled over the Chola, Kalinga and Pandiya countries. (Comparative Grammar, Introd. p. 136.)

The language of the Moors is Tamil but is saturated with Arabic as the Dravida is with Sanscrit, and as the languages of the Christian communities of Ceylon and India are, with Biblical names of persons and rites.

Although the first armed irruption of the Mahommadans into the Deccan did not take place till A. D. 1294 when Alla-ad-din crossed the Nerbudda and swept the whole country without molestation for 25 days, yet it must not be supposed that they were unknown in Ceylon before. For Marco Polo, (A. D. 1291), says that the Singhalese were averse to a military life, and they got their soldiers from the Mahommedans.

---

## THE COLOMBO CHETTIES.

These people are a branch of the Tamil race and are distinguished from the rest of it by their dress and religion. Tradition does not assign a more distant date than the middle of the 16th century to their migration into Ceylon. Before that period, they had frequently visited Ceylon for purposes of trade: their original seat was Tinnavelli, a different district from whence Jaffna was colonized. The name, by which they are known, is that of their caste, namely "the Chetti", one of the sub-divisions of the Vaisiya caste. And the Vaisiya caste holds the third place among the four main castes into which the Hindu Shastras divide the human race, namely the Brahman, Kshatri, Vasiya and Sudra, of which, the first three are ranked as high castes, and the last as servile.

High caste women never go beyond the limits of their respective districts, much less cross over the sea. The Chetti traders accordingly came alone and occasionally formed matrimonial alliances among the high caste natives of the neighbourhood of Colombo, Thoppu, and Munnesuram. They, nevertheless, kept up their national religion, dress, customs and language, until the conquest of the Portuguese, when they embraced the religion of the conquerors, finding that that was the readiest means to preferment and protection from oppression. Having once embraced the Catholic faith, the direst persecution could not move them from it. With a tenacity, which is characteristic of the caste, they preserve their new religion with the same jealousy with which they still preserve their unique dress, ancient customs and social observances. At the end of the 16th century owing to a great famine in Southern India, numbers of new Chetties came to Ceylon bringing, however, with them their wives and daughters, impelled, it must be presumed, by hunger, to break through the traditionary dignity of their caste. The new arrivals embraced the religion of the older and more prosperous settlers of their caste, and by forming intermarriages soon became one with them. The faith of the Chettis in their new religion stood the test of a 150 years of persecution during the Dutch period, and the late Kanjamanatha Muthaliyar, himself a Chetti and a Catholic, dwells with pride, in his Vinea Taprobanea, on the religious fervour of the caste during those troublous times. A few families however became protestant during the Dutch period and they remain so up to this day.

But the Chetties, whether Catholic, Protestant or Saivite, acknowledge a common tie, the tie of Caste, and unite together on occasions of domestic festivities.

By the law of caste, as understood among the Hindus, a man of a superior caste is allowed to take a wife from an inferior immediately next to his; and the offspring of such a marriage retains the condition of the father. On the other hand the offspring, of a woman, procreated by one who is inferior to her in caste is an outcaste. Accordingly the Chettis have frequently availed themselves of the privilege and married women of the Bhu-vaisiya or Vellala (i. e. agricultural) caste, but they scrupulously abstain from marrying out their daughters to any one but a Chetti. Nevertheless education, European civilization, and the possession of wealth have effected considerable relaxation in these matters.

## THE TAMILS OF JAFFNA.

Little more is known of these people than is contained in the Vaipavamalai.

Of the lutist who founded the colony, the following account is given by Casie Chetty in his Tamil Plutarch, (p.p. 118—9 )

" Yalpana Nayanar, otherwise called Viraragaven, was a minstrel who lived in the Chola country. Being blind, he depended for his subsistence entirely on the earnings of his wife. One day his wife having delayed to serve out to him his meals at the proper hour, he quarrelled with her on that account, and quitted his house, saying, that he was going to Ceylon, upon which she sneeringly observed. "Ah! you are going to Ceylon to obtain a tusked elephant and a fertile land." When he arrived in Ceylon, he was refused admittance into the king's presence, as it was considered ominous for a king to see a blind man; but it was afterwards arranged that the king should stand behind a curtain, and hear the blind minstrel's song. The king divesting himself of his royal garments, put on a pair of short drawers like those worn by an archer, and stood behind the curtain with a bow in his hand, and bade him sing. He some how or other, being informed of the king's disguise improvised the following stanza characterizing the king as Rama of old :—

*O Aditya !* (meaning Rama) *whose potent arms stemmed the waves of the sea, pray why have thy hands assumed the bow ? for, the prosperous Lanka has neither her king* (meaning Ravana), *nor the stag* (meaning Marichi,) who in the disguise of a stag decoyed away Rama from Sita), *nor the seven Mara trees* (meaning those which Rama shot through with a single arrow) *to shoot at ?.*

The king immediately laid aside the garb of the archer, and successively putting on the robes of the Queen, and his own, desired him to sing. He thereupon composed extempore a lyric in ten stanzas to suit the respective guises of the king, and sang it to the lute which he himself played. The king being greatly pleased with his performance, honored him with the gift of a tusked elephant, and by the donation of a land on the northern extremity of the Island in perpetuity; and thus was realized what his wife had said in bitter irony.

The land which he obtained from the king was no other than the present peninsula of Jaffna. It was then uninhabited, and covered with jungle, but he had it cleared, and having induced a colony of Tamils from Southern India to settle in it, soon rendered it a rich country which he called after his own professional name Yalpana nadu i.e., the minstrel's country. He did not, however, assume any sovereignty over the country, but inviting over from the Continent a youth, who was the natural son of a Chola king by a Brahaman woman, installed him as its king, under the title of Singariya Chakravarti. The installation of Singariya Chakravarti is stated in the Kailasa Malei to have occurred in the Kali year 3000 (A. D. 101); and if this date be correct, the Singhalese monarch, who patronized the minstrel, must have been Wasabha, who reigned at Anuradhapura from A. D. 62 to 106. In the lyric, which has been noticed above, the minstrel does not celebrate his patron under his proper name, he styles him merely Pararajasingan, an appellation signifying one who is as a lion to other kings."

This account slightly differs from that given in the Vaipavamalai. But tradition supports the Vaipavamalai and asserts that the lutist did assume sovereignty and that a considerable time had elapsed from the death of the lutist before Ariyachchakkravarthi vaulted into the vacant throne of Jaffna.

Be this as it may, there can be no doubt that two bodies of colonists were led into Ceylon at different times, one by the lutist and the other by the Chakkravarthi. The descendants of the latter who were all men of good birth and substance in their own country, despise up to this day those of the lutist's colonists, and cast it in their teeth that their ancestors had been "picked in broad day before they had been shipped."

The following tradition explains the satire.

When the Cholan gave permission to his subjects to migrate into Ceylon, his minister represented to him that large numbers of them were intending to avail themselves of the permission. Thereupon the king and his minister posted themselves by the side of a sheet of water which the emigrants had to wade through, in order to reach the boats that the lutist had ready to convey them to the ships. In crossing the water some women tucked up the cloths they had on up to an indecent height. Others, through modesty, would not so much as raise their cloths above their ankles. The modest women were sent back to their homes with their husbands and children, and only the families of the immodest women were permitted to follow the lutist. Hence the disgrace which is said to attach to the early colonists, in the eyes of those who accompanied the Chakkravarthi.

# THE PAGNCHANKAM

OR

# THE TAMIL CALENDAR.

1. The Tamils count four ages or *Yugas* of the world. The first consisted of 1,728,000 years; the second of 1,296,000; and the third of 864,000. The fourth, *Kaliyuga*, or the age of poverty, consists of 432,000 years. We are at present living in the *Kaliyuga*, of which the year 4,979 ended on Friday the 12th of April, 1878, A.D., at 1 hour and 45 minutes A.M.

2. The Tamils seldom employ the *Kaliyuga* year in recording civil transactions or historical events. For these purposes they use a list or cycle of sixty names from which they name their years in unbroken succession. And as often as the sixty names are exhausted, they begin the list over again and go on to the end.*

---

* The curious reader will find much valuable information on the ancient Hindu Calendar in Colebrooke's Essays on the Religion and Philosophy of the Hindus. (pp. 65—67.)

3. The following are the names of the sixty years :—

1. Pirapava.
2. Vipava.
3. Sukkila.
4. Piramóthûtha.
5. Pirasótpaththi
6. Angkírasa.
7. Srímuka.
8. Pava.
9. Uva.
10. Thatu.
11. Isura.
12. Vekuthániya.
13. Pirámathi.
14. Vikkirama.
15. Visu.
16. Siththirapanu.
17. Supánu.
18. Tárana.
19. Párththiva.
20. Viya.
21. Sarvasiththi.
22. Sarvatari.
23. Virothi.
24. Vikirthi.
25. Kara.
26. Nanthana.
27. Visaya.
28. Jaya.
29. Manmatha.
30. Thurmuki.
31. Evilampi.
32. Vilampi.
33. Vikári.
34. Sarvari.
35. Pilava.
36. Supakiruthu.
37. Sópakiruthu.
38. Kuróthi.
39. Visuvávasu.
40. Parápava.
41. Pilavanka.
42. Kilaka.
43. Saumiya.
44. Sáthárana.
45. Viróthikiruthu.
46. Parithávi.
47. Piramáthísa.
48. Anantha.
49. Irádchatha
50. Nala.
51. Pingkala.
52. Kálayuththi.
53. Siththárthi.
54. Irauththiri.
55. Thurmathi.
56. Thunthupi.
57. Ruthirótcári.
58. Iraththádchi.
59. Kuróthana.
60. Adchaya

4. To guard against a year of one cycle being mistaken for a year of the same name in a preceding or a succeeding, cycle, the Tamils employ the era of King *Salivakanan.* This era is usually termed the *Salivakana Sakaptham*, or briefly the *Saka* year. According to the Rajavali (p. 226) the *Saka* year took its date from the fate of a Brahmana woman who starved herself to death in order to escape the wicked intention of a King. Its first year commenced in a *Vekuthaniya* year (the 12th year of the cycle) and corresponds as shall be shewn hereafter, with A. D. 78.

For example, a Tamil would say "This event took place in the year *Isura* which is passing beyond *Salivakana Saka* year 1799." The meaning of this expression is that the year 1799 *Saka* is entirely past, and the year *Isura* corresponds with the *Saka* year 1800. Accordingly, it is necessary to bear in mind that in a Tamil expression, the cyclic year which is *named* therein corresponds, not with the *Saka* year represented by the numerals by the side of which that cyclic year stands, but with the *Saka* year that follows it.

5. In expressing dates, Tamil authors sometimes give both the *Saka* year and the *cyclic* name and sometimes the *cyclic* name only. Where the *cyclic* year alone is expressed, it is impossible to determine the date of an occurrence. Where the Saka year is given, we can convert a date into its corresponding date in the English calendar. But the process is a matter of no small difficulty, and the following paragraphs will, it is hoped, be of assistance to those who have occasion to convert English dates into Tamil, and *vice versa.*

6. The Tamils have but one year, whether it be for civil, historical, or astronomical purposes. That year is of a uniform length and consists of 52 weeks, 1 day, 15 *nadi*, 31 *vinadi*, and 15 *thatparai*. It begins when the sun enters (according to Tamil calculation) the first point of Aries. For the sake of brevity, weeks, days, *nadi*, *vinadi*, and *thatparai* will be respectively indicated by their initials, *w. d. n. v.* and *t.* A week consists of 7 days, a day of 60 *nadi*, a *nadi* of 60 *vinadi* ; and a *vinadi* of 60 *thatparai*.

7. The Tamil calendar makes use of no intercalations. It avoids them by commencing its new year exactly where it considers the old year ends, according to astronomical calcula-

tions. This method is not without its inconvenience, for, the year seldom begins at the same moment at which the day begins, and few men are able to carry on the calculations which are necessary to fix the beginning of a given year. Other inconveniences will appear in the sequel.

8. There are seven days in the week. Their names and significations are :

| | | | |
|---|---|---|---|
| 1. | Gnáyiru | ... ... ... | Sunday-Monday. |
| 2. | Thingkal | ... ... ... | Monday-Tuesday. |
| 3. | Sevváy | ... ... ... | Tuesday-Wednesday. |
| 4. | Puthan | ... ... ... | Wednesday-Thursday. |
| 5. | Viyálan | ... ... ... | Thursday-Friday. |
| 6. | Velli... | ... ... ... | Friday-Saturday. |
| 7. | Sani | ... ... ... | Saturday-Sunday. |

The European day is reckoned from midnight to midnight, but the *Tamil* day is reckoned from sunrise to sunrise. Hence the *Tamil Gnayiru*, for instance, does not begin before sunrise on the European Sunday. The same remark applies to the other days.

9. There are twelve months in the year. Their names, significations, and lengths are :

| | | D. | N. | V. | T. |
|---|---|---|---|---|---|
| 1. | Siththirai or Médam = Ram ... ... ... | 30 | 55 | 32 | 00 |
| 2. | Vaikási or Idapam =Bull ... ... ... | 31 | 24 | 12 | 00 |
| 3. | A'ni or Mithunam = Gemini ... ... ... | 31 | 36 | 38 | 00 |
| 4. | A'di or Katkadakam = Crab ... ... ... | 31 | 28 | 12 | 00 |
| 5. | A'vani or Singkam = Lion ... ... ... | 31 | 2 | 10 | 00 |
| 6. | Puraddási or Kanni = Virgin ... ... ... | 30 | 27 | 22 | 00 |
| 7. | Atpasi or Thulam = Balance ... ... ... | 29 | 54 | 7 | 00 |
| 8. | Kárththikai or Virudchikam=Scorpion ... | 29 | 30 | 24 | 00 |
| 9. | Márkali or Thanusu=Bow ... ... ... | 29 | 20 | 53 | 00 |
| 10. | Thai or Makaram=Shark ... ... ... | 29 | 27 | 16 | 00 |
| 11. | Mási or Kumpam=Pot ... ... ... | 29 | 48 | 24 | 00 |
| 12. | Pangkuni or Mínam=Fish ... ... ... | 30 | 20 | 21 | 15 |
| | | 365 | 15 | 31 | 15 |

As in the case of the year, so does each month run on until its last *vinadi* or *thatparai* is fully past. Exactly at the *punctum* of time when a given month ends, its successor begins, without any regard being had to the time of day or night when the ending or beginning takes place.

However, when the commencement of a month happens to fall after sunset and before sunrise, the first date of that month is marked in the *Pagnchangkam* as if it took place at the sunrise which follows the commencement of the month. The second, third, and subsequent days will likewise be marked as taking place at sunrise. But this is merely a convenient form of marking dates. The fraction of the night between the true beginning of the month and its first sunrise is never lost sight of, for, the end of the month is determined with reference to its true beginning, and not to the time when its first or last date is marked, on the *Pagnchangkam*, as having commenced.

10. To find the beginning of a Tamil year,

Take a *Pagnchangkam*, say for the year *Isura*, which corresponds with the *Saka* year, 1,800. On turning to the page devoted to its last month, the last two lines will be found to contain the following information, namely, that:

1st.—*Isura* ends at 49 N. 22 V., on *Viyala* day the 31st of *Pangkuni*.

2nd.—The 31st day of *Pangkuni* begins on Thursday the 11th of April, 1878.

3rd.—At the exact minute at which *Isura* ends its successor *Vekuthaniya* commences.

Now, as according to the European way of reckoning days, the 11th of April commences, roughly speaking, fifteen *nalikai* before *Viyalan* commences, so, when the *Tamil* speak of 49 N. 22 V., of *Viyala* day, they mean 4 N. 22 V., A.M., of Friday the 12th of April of the Europeans.

And, for reasons stated in the preceding paragraph, the interval between the 4 N. 22 V. and the sunrise of the 12th of April is reckoned (merely for purposes of recording dates) as forming part of the last date of the dying year, though for all other purposes, the year commences at 4 N. 22 V., A.M., of the European Friday, the 12th of April, 1878, A.D.

11. The *Pagnchangam* usually disregards *thatparai*, and accordingly the 30 *thatparai* have been omitted in exhibiting the end of the *Isura* year. *Isura* properly ends at 4 N. 22 V. 30 T., A.M., on the 12th of April, 1878, A.D.

12. The commencement of a Tamil year with its corresponding English dates will be exhibited in these pages in the following form:—

| | | | | D. | N. | V. | T. | |
|---|---|---|---|---|---|---|---|---|
| Saka | 1801 | = A.D. 1878 | April | 11 | 4 | 22 | 30 | Vekuthaniya. |

The meaning of this expression is that when the *Saka* year 1801, (whose cyclic name is *Vekuthaniya*), commenced, there were fully past 11 D. 4 N. 22 V. 30 T. in the month of April 1878, *i.e.*, as has been before explained, the year commenced on the 12th of April at 4 N. 22 V. 30 T., A.M.

13. To find the commencement of a future year, one has only to add the length of the Tamil year to the commencement of the last ascertained Tamil year, and the sum will give the commencement of the succeeding year.

To find the corresponding English date of the commencement of the Tamil year, deduct from the above sum 365 days, when the Saka year passes through a common year, or 366 days when it passes through a leap year. As for instance:—

| | D. | N. | V. | T. | |
|---|---|---|---|---|---|
| To Saka Year 1801 = A.D. 1878, April | 11 | 4 | 22 | 30 | Vekuthaniya. |
| Add ... | 365 | 15 | 31 | 15 | |
| Total... | 376 | 19 | 53 | 45 | |
| From this total deduct | 365 | | | | |
| Which leaves a difference of | 11 | 19 | 53 | 45 | |

This difference shews the hour when the *Saka* year 1802 commences, *i.e.*, it commences on the 12th of April, A.D., 1879 at 19 N. 53 V. 45 T. A.M. This result with the cyclic name of the year, namely *Piramathi*, will be found registered in the *Pagnchangkam*, thus, *Piramathi* which is now passing after the completion of the *Saka* year 1801 commences on April 12th at 4 N. 53 V. and 45 T. after sunrise, *i.e.*, assuming that the sun rises exactly at 6 hours after midnight.

In like manner to find the commencement of the next year.

| | D. | N. | V. | T. | |
|---|---|---|---|---|---|
| Saka 1802 = A. D. 1879, April | 11 | 19 | 53 | 45 | Piramathi. |
| Add ... ... | 365 | 15 | 31 | 15 | |
| Total... | 376 | 35 | 25 | 00 | |

Deduct 366, as Piramathi passes through the February of 1880 which is an intercalary month.

The difference 10 D. 35 N. 25 V. shows that the *Saka* year 1803 (whose name is found on the cycle to be *Vikkirama*) commences after 10 D. 35 N. and 25 V. are fully past in April, 1880, A.D.

This result will be found registered in the *Pagnchangkam* thus: The year *Vikkirama* which passes after the completion of the *Saka* year 1802 commences on April 11, 1880, A.D., at 20 N. 25 V. after sunrise.

14. To find the commencement of the first year of the *Sakaptham*.

| | D. | N. | V. | T. |
|---|---|---|---|---|
| By the *Pagnchangkam* the Saka year 1800 ends in A.D. 1878 ... ... ...April | 11 | 4 | 22 | 30 |
| In March, February and January of A.D. 1878, there were ... ... ... ... | 90 | 00 | 00 | 00 |
| From the end of 1877 to the beginning of A.D. 1753 there were 125 years of 365 days each with 30 intercalary days ... ... ... | 45655 | 00 | 00 | 00 |
| In A.D. 1752 there were so far as the English were concerned... ... ... ... ... | 355 | 00 | 00 | 00 |
| From the end of A.D. 1751 to the beginning of A.D. 79 there were 1673 years of 365 days each with 418 intercalary days ... ... | 611063 | 00 | 00 | 00 |
| From December 31st A.D. 78 to March 1st A, D, 78 there were ... ... ... ... ... | 306 | 00 | 00 | 00 |
| Total... | 657480 | 4 | 22 | 30 |

Now as the length of the *Tamil* year is 365 D. 15 N. 31 V. 15 T. and as 1800 such years have passed since the commencement of the *Sakaptham* the time that has expired up to A. D. 1878 April 11th 4 D. 22 V. 30 N. is 657,465 D. 37 N. 30 V. 0 T.

| | D. | N. | V. | T. |
|---|---|---|---|---|
| Now from ... | 657480 | 4 | 22 | 30 |
| Subtract ... | 657465 | 37 | 30 | 00 |
| The difference is | 14 | 26 | 52 | 30 |

This difference means that the *Salivakana Sakaptham* commenced on the 15th day of March A.D. 78, at 26 N. 52 V. 30 T A.M. This same thing would be found registered in the

*Pagnchangam*, if there had been a pagnchangam for that year, thus "A.D. 78, March 15th 11 N. 52 V. 30 T. *Vekuthania*."

By a similar process of recession from 1878 all the intermediate years may be easily found and registered.

It is necessary that the reader should be here apprized that the cyclic form of computation did not commence till 349 years after the *Sakaptham* commenced. So that from Saka 1 to Saka 349 the years had no name, and writers living in those days could only have indicated them by their number. But for the sake of uniformity of expression later writers assign cyclic names to those years when they have occasion to speak of them.

The following table contains a few of the Saka years with their commencements :—

### 15.—*The Beginning of Tamil Years.*

| Saka or Tamil Years. | | Equal to A.D. | | | D. | N. | V. | T. | |
|---|---|---|---|---|---|---|---|---|---|
| 1801 | ... | 1878 | April | ... | 11 | 4 | 22 | 30 | Vekuthániya |
| 1800 | ... | 1877 | April | ... | 10 | 48 | 51 | 15 | Isura |
| 1799 | ... | 1876 | April | ... | 10 | 33 | 20 | 00 | Tháthu |
| 1798 | ... | 1875 | April | ... | 11 | 17 | 48 | 45 | Yuva |
| 1797 | ... | 1874 | April | .. | 11 | 2 | 17 | 30 | Pava |
| 1796 | ... | 1873 | April | ... | 10 | 46 | 46 | 15 | Srimuka |
| 1795 | ... | 1872 | April | ... | 10 | 31 | 15 | 00 | Ankírasa |
| 1794 | ... | 1871 | April | ... | 11 | 15 | 43 | 45 | Pirasótpathi |
| 1793 | ... | 1870 | April | ... | 11 | 00 | 12 | 30 | Piramothutha |
| 1792 | ... | 1869 | April | ... | 10 | 44 | 41 | 15 | Sukkila |
| 1791 | ... | 1868 | April | ... | 10 | 29 | 10 | 00 | Vipava |
| 1790 | ... | 1867 | April | ... | 11 | 13 | 38 | 45 | Pirapava |
| 1789 | ... | 1866 | April | ... | 10 | 58 | 7 | 30 | Adchaya |
| 1788 | ... | 1865 | April | ... | 10 | 42 | 36 | 15 | Kuróthana |
| 1787 | ... | 1864 | April | ... | 10 | 27 | 5 | 00 | Iraththádchi |
| 1786 | ... | 1863 | April | ... | 11 | 11 | 33 | 45 | Ruthirótkári |

| Saka or Tamil Years. | | Equal to A.D. | | | D. | N. | V. | T. | |
|---|---|---|---|---|---|---|---|---|---|
| 1785 | ... | 1862 | April | ... | 10 | 56 | 2 | 30 | Thunthupi |
| 1784 | ... | 1861 | April | ... | 10 | 40 | 31 | 15 | Thunmathi |
| 1783 | ... | 1860 | April | ... | 10 | 25 | 00 | 00 | Irauththiri |
| 1782 | ... | 1859 | April | ... | 11 | 9 | 28 | 45 | Siththarththi |
| 1781 | ... | 1858 | April | .. | 10 | 53 | 57 | 30 | Kalayuththi |
| 1780 | ... | 1857 | April | ... | 10 | 38 | 26 | 15 | Pingkala |
| 1779 | ... | 1856 | April | ... | 10 | 22 | 55 | 00 | Nala |
| 1778 | ... | 1855 | April | ... | 11 | 7 | 23 | 45 | Iradchatha |
| 1777 | ... | 1854 | April | ... | 10 | 51 | 52 | 30 | Anantha |
| 1776 | ... | 1853 | April | ... | 10 | 36 | 21 | 15 | Piramathisa |
| 1775 | ... | 1852 | April | ... | 10 | 20 | 50 | 00 | Parithavi |
| 1774 | ... | 1851 | April | ... | 11 | 5 | 18 | 45 | Virothikiruthu |
| 1773 | ... | 1850 | April | ... | 10 | 49 | 47 | .30 | Sathárana |
| 1772 | ... | 1849 | April | ... | 10 | 34 | 16 | 15 | Saumiya |
| 1771 | ... | 1848 | April | ... | 10 | 18 | 45 | 00 | Kílaka |
| 1770 | ... | 1847 | April | ... | 11 | 3 | 13 | 45 | Pilavangka |
| 1769 | ... | 1846 | April | ... | 10 | 47 | 42 | 30 | Parápava |
| 1768 | ... | 1845 | April | ... | 10 | 32 | 11 | 15 | Visuvavasu |
| 1767 | ... | 1844 | April | ... | 10 | 16 | 40 | 00 | Kurothi |
| 1766 | ... | 1843 | April | ... | 11 | 1 | 8 | 45 | Sópakiruthu |
| 1765 | ... | 1842 | April | ... | 10 | 45 | 37 | 30 | Supakiruthu |
| 1764 | ... | 1841 | April | ... | 10 | 30 | 6 | 15 | Pilawa |
| 1763 | ... | 1840 | April | ... | 10 | 14 | 35 | 00 | Sárvari |
| 1762 | ... | 1839 | April | ... | 10 | 59 | 3 | 45 | Vikári |
| 1761 | ... | 1838 | April | ... | 10 | 43 | 32 | 30 | Vilampi |
| 1760 | ... | 1837 | April | ... | 10 | 28 | 1 | 15 | Evilampi |
| 1759 | ... | 1836 | April | ... | 10 | 12 | 30 | 00 | Thurmuki |
| 1758 | ... | 1835 | April | ... | 10 | 56 | 58 | 45 | Manmatha |
| 1757 | ... | 1834 | April | ... | 10 | 41 | 27 | 30 | Jaya |
| 1756 | ... | 1833 | April | ... | 10 | 25 | 56 | 15 | Visaya |
| 1755 | ... | 1832 | April | ... | 10 | 10 | 25 | 00 | Nanthana |
| 1754 | ... | 1831 | April | ... | 10 | 54 | 53 | 45 | Kara |
| 1753 | ... | 1830 | April | ... | 10 | 39 | 22 | 30 | Vikirthi |
| 1752 | ... | 1829 | April | ... | 10 | 23 | 51 | 15 | Virothi |
| 1751 | ... | 1828 | April | ... | 10 | 8 | 20 | 00 | Sarvathári |
| 1750 | ... | 1827 | April | ... | 10 | 52 | 48 | 45 | Sarvasiththi |
| 1749 | ... | 1826 | April | .. | 10 | 37 | 17 | 30 | Viya |
| 1748 | ... | 1825 | April | .. | 10 | 21 | 46 | 15 | Parthiva |
| 1747 | ... | 1824 | April | ... | 10 | 6 | 15 | 00 | Thárana |
| 1746 | .. | 1823 | April | ... | 10 | 50 | 43 | 45 | Supánu |
| 1745 | ... | 1822 | April | ... | 10 | 35 | 12 | 30 | Siththirapánu |
| 1744 | ... | 1821 | April | ... | 10 | 19 | 41 | 15 | Visu |
| 1743 | ... | 1820 | April | ... | 10 | 4 | 10 | 00 | Vikkirama |

| Saka or Tamil Years. | | Equal to A.D. | | | D. | N | V. | T. | |
|---|---|---|---|---|---|---|---|---|---|
| 1742 | ... | 1819 | April | ... | 10 | 48 | 38 | 45 | Piramáthi |
| 1741 | ... | 1818 | April | ... | 10 | 33 | 7 | 30 | Vekuthániya |
| 1740 | ... | 1817 | April | ... | 10 | 17 | 36 | 15 | Isura |
| 1739 | ... | 1816 | April | ... | 10 | 2 | 5 | 00 | Thathu |
| 1738 | ... | 1815 | April | ... | 10 | 46 | 33 | 45 | Yuva |
| 1737 | ... | 1814 | April | ... | 10 | 31 | 2 | 30 | Pava |
| 1736 | ... | 1813 | April | ... | 10 | 15 | 31 | 15 | Srimuka |
| 1735 | .. | 1812 | April | ... | 10 | 00 | 00 | 00 | Angkírasa |
| 1734 | .. | 1811 | April | .. | 10 | 44 | 28 | 45 | Pirasótpathi |
| 1733 | ... | 1810 | April | ... | 10 | 28 | 57 | 30 | Piramothutha |
| 1732 | ... | 1809 | April | ... | 10 | 13 | 26 | 15 | Sukkila |
| 1731 | ... | 1808 | April | ... | 9 | 57 | 55 | 00 | Vipava |
| 1730 | ... | 1807 | April | ... | 10 | 42 | 23 | 45 | Pirapava |
| 1729 | ... | 1806 | April | ... | 10 | 26 | 52 | 30 | Adchaya |
| 1728 | ... | 1805 | April | ... | 10 | 11 | 21 | 15 | Kuróthana |
| 1727 | ... | 1804 | April | ... | 9 | 55 | 50 | 00 | Iraththádchi |
| 1726 | ... | 1803 | April | ... | 10 | 40 | 18 | 45 | Ruthirótkàri |
| 1725 | ... | 1802 | April | ... | 10 | 24 | 47 | 30 | Thunthupi |
| 1724 | ... | 1801 | April | ... | 10 | 9 | 16 | 15 | Thurmathi |
| 1723 | ... | 1800 | April | ... | 9 | 53 | 45 | 00 | Irauththiri |
| 1722 | ... | 1799 | April | ... | 9 | 38 | 13 | 45 | Siththarthi |
| 1721 | ... | 1798 | April | ... | 9 | 22 | 42 | 30 | Kálayuththi |
| 1720 | ... | 1797 | April | ... | 9 | 7 | 11 | 15 | Pingkala |
| 1719 | ... | 1796 | April | ... | 8 | 51 | 40 | 00 | Nala |
| 1718 | ... | 1795 | April | ... | 9 | 36 | 8 | 45 | Iràdchatha |
| 1717 | ... | 1794 | April | ... | 9 | 20 | 37 | 30 | Anantha |
| 1716 | ... | 1793 | April | ... | 9 | 5 | 6 | 15 | Piramathisa |
| 1715 | ... | 1792 | April | ... | 8 | 49 | 35 | 00 | Parithavi. |
| 1714 | ... | 1791 | April | ... | 9 | 34 | 3 | 45 | Virothikiruthu. |
| 1713 | ... | 1790 | April | ... | 9 | 18 | 32 | 30 | Sâthàrana. |
| 1712 | ... | 1789 | April | ... | 9 | 3 | 1 | 15 | Saumiya. |
| 1711 | ... | 1788 | April | ... | 8 | 47 | 30 | 00 | Kilaka. |
| 1710 | ... | 1787 | April | ... | 9 | 31 | 58 | 45 | Pelavangka. |
| 1709 | ... | 1786 | April | ... | 9 | 16 | 27 | 30 | Parpava. |
| 1708 | ... | 1785 | April | ... | 9 | 00 | 56 | 15 | Visuvàvasu. |
| 1707 | ... | 1784 | April | ... | 8 | 45 | 25 | 00 | Kuròthi. |
| 1706 | ... | 1783 | April | ... | 9 | 29 | 53 | 45 | Sòpakiruthu. |
| 1705 | ... | 1782 | April | ... | 9 | 14 | 22 | 30 | Supakiruthu. |
| 1704 | ... | 1781 | April | ... | 8 | 58 | 51 | 15 | Pilava. |
| 1703 | ... | 1780 | April | ... | 8 | 43 | 20 | 00 | Sàrvari. |
| 1702 | ... | 1779 | April | ... | 9 | 27 | 48 | 45 | Vikàri. |
| 1701 | ... | 1778 | April | ... | 9 | 12 | 17 | 30 | Vilampi. |
| 1700 | ... | 1777 | April | ... | 8 | 56 | 46 | 15 | Evilampi. |

| Saka or Tamil Years. | | Equal to A.D. | | | D. | N. | V. | T. | |
|---|---|---|---|---|---|---|---|---|---|
| 1699 | ... | 1776 | April | ... | 8 | 41 | 15 | 00 | Thurmuki. |
| 1698 | ... | 1775 | April | ... | 9 | 25 | 43 | 45 | Manmatha. |
| 1697 | ... | 1774 | April | ... | 9 | 10 | 12 | 30 | Jaya, |
| 1696 | ... | 1773 | April | ... | 8 | 54 | 41 | 15 | Visaya, |
| 1695 | ... | 1772 | April | ... | 8 | 39 | 10 | 00 | Nanthana |
| 1694 | ... | 1771 | April | ... | 9 | 23 | 38 | 45 | Kara |
| 1693 | ... | 1770 | April | ... | 9 | 8 | 7 | 30 | Vikirthi |
| 1692 | ... | 1769 | April | ... | 8 | 52 | 36 | 15 | Viróthi |
| 1691 | ... | 1768 | April | ... | 8 | 37 | 5 | 00 | Sarvathàri |
| 1690 | ... | 1767 | April | ... | 9 | 21 | 33 | 45 | Sarvasiththu |
| 1689 | ... | 1766 | April | ... | 9 | 6 | 2 | 30 | Viya |
| 1688 | ... | 1765 | April | ... | 8 | 50 | 31 | 15 | Parththiva |
| 1687 | ... | 1764 | April | ... | 8 | 35 | 00 | 00 | Thárana |
| 1686 | ... | 1763 | April | ... | 9 | 19 | 28 | 45 | Supânu |
| 1685 | ... | 1762 | April | ... | 9 | 3 | 57 | 30 | Siththirapánu |
| 1684 | ... | 1761 | April | ... | 8 | 48 | 26 | 15 | Visu |
| 1683 | ... | 1760 | April | ... | 8 | 32 | 55 | 00 | Vikkirama |
| 1682 | ... | 1759 | April | ... | 9 | 17 | 23 | 45 | Piramathi |
| 1681 | ... | 1758 | April | ... | 9 | 1 | 52 | 30 | Vekuthaniya |
| 1680 | ... | 1757 | April | ... | 8 | 46 | 21 | 15 | Isura |
| 1679 | ... | 1756 | April | ... | 8 | 30 | 50 | 00 | Thathu |
| 1678 | ... | 1755 | April | ... | 9 | 15 | 18 | 45 | Yuva |
| 1677 | ... | 1754 | April | ... | 8 | 59 | 47 | 30 | Pava |
| 1676 | ... | 1753 | April | ... | 8 | 44 | 16 | 15 | Srimuka |
| 1675 | ... | 1752 | March | ... | 28 | 28 | 45 | 00 | Angkirasa. The September of this year had only 19 days in Great Britain. |
| 1674 | ... | 1751 | March | ... | 29 | 13 | 13 | 45 | Pirasótpathi |
| 1673 | ... | 1750 | March | ... | 28 | 57 | 42 | 30 | Piramóthutha |
| 1672 | ... | 1749 | March | ... | 28 | 42 | 11 | 15 | Sukkila |
| 1671 | ... | 1748 | March | ... | 28 | 26 | 40 | 00 | Vipava |
| 1670 | ... | 1747 | March | ... | 29 | 11 | 8 | 45 | Pirapava |

16. The year when Great Britain adopted the Gregorian change is A.D. 1752, therefore beyond A.D. 1752, the process of recession is simple. But it must be recollected that the Portuguese introduced that change into Ceylon in 1581 and read the 5th of October as the 15th of that month.

17. A *Tamil* year is longer than the Julian Common year by 15 N. 31 V. 15 T., and shorter than the Leap year by 44 N. 28 V. 45 T. Accordingly, in four years, the difference will be 2 N. and 5 V. In 60 years, 31 N. 15 V. In a 100 years 52 N. 5 V. These figures or their multiples subtracted from, or (if the case required) added, to the beginning of a known year, will give the beginning of a required year.

Hence, for examples, from 1670 of the *Sakaptham* we deduce the following years :—

| Tamil Years. | Equal to A.D. | | D. | N. | V. | T. | |
|---|---|---|---|---|---|---|---|
| 1670... | 1747 | March ... | 29 | 11 | 8 | 45 | Pirapava. |
| | | | | 2 | 5 | 00 | deduction for four years. |
| 1666... | 1743 | March ... | 29 | 9 | 3 | 45 | Ruthirotkári. |
| | | | | 46 | 33 | 45 | deduction for three common years |
| 1663... | 1740 | March ... | 28 | 22 | 30 | 00 | Irauththiri. |
| | | | | 52 | 5 | 00 | deduction for one hundred years |
| 1563... | 1640 | March ... | 27 | 30 | 25 | 00 | Vikkirama. |
| | | | 2 | 36 | 15 | 00 | deduction for three hundred years |
| 1263... | 1340 | March ... | 24 | 54 | 10 | 00 | Vikkirama. |
| | | | | 44 | 28 | 45 | addition for a leap year |
| 1262... | 1339 | March ... | 25 | 38 | 38 | 45 | Piramatni. |
| | | | | 15 | 31 | 15 | deduction for a common year |
| 1261... | 1338 | March ... | 25 | 23 | 7 | 30 | Vekuthaniya. |
| | | | | 13 | 26 | 15 | addition for two common years and one Leap year. |
| 1258... | 1335 | March ... | 25 | 36 | 33 | 45 | Yuva. |
| | | | | 31 | 15 | 00 | deduction for 60 years |

| Tamil Years. | Equal to A.D. | | D. | N. | V. | T. | |
|---|---|---|---|---|---|---|---|
| 1198 | 1275 | March ... | 25 | 5 | 18 | 45 | Yuva. |
| | | | | 20 | 50 | 00 | deduction for forty years. |
| 1158 | 1235 | March ... | 24 | 44 | 28 | 45 | Manmatha. |
| | | | | 10 | 25 | 00 | deduction for twenty years. |
| 1138 | 1215 | March ... | 24 | 34 | 3 | 45 | Yuva. |
| | | | | 4 | 10 | 00 | deduction for eight years. |
| 1130 | 1207 | March ... | 24 | 29 | 53 | 45 | Pirapava. |
| | | | 5 | 12 | 30 | 00 | deduction for six hundred years. |
| 530 | 607 | March ... | 19 | 17 | 23 | 45 | Pirapava, |
| | | | | 8 | 20 | 00 | deduction for sixteen years. |
| 514 | 591 | March ... | 19 | 9 | 3 | 45 | Supanu. |
| | | | | 31 | 2 | 30 | deduction for two common years. |
| 512 | 589 | March ... | 18 | 38 | 1 | 15 | Parthiva. |
| | | | 2 | 36 | 15 | 00 | deduction for three hundred years. |
| 212 | 289 | March ... | 16 | 1 | 46 | 15 | Parthiva. |
| | | | 1 | 2 | 30 | 30 | deduction for one hundred and twenty years. |
| 92 | 169 | March ... | 14 | 59 | 16 | 15 | Parthiva. |
| | | | | 20 | 50 | 00 | deduction for forty years. |
| 52 | 129 | March ... | 14 | 38 | 26 | 15 | Kurothana. |
| | | | | 15 | 31 | 15 | deduction for a common year. |
| 51 | 128 | March ... | 14 | 22 | 55 | 00 | Adchaya. |
| | | | | 44 | 28 | 45 | addition for a leap year. |
| 50 | 127 | March ... | 15 | 7 | 23 | 45 | Pirapava. |
| | | | | 4 | 10 | 10 | deduction for eight years. |
| 42 | 119 | March ... | 15 | 3 | 13 | 45 | Siththarththi. |
| | | | | 20 | 50 | 00 | deduction for forty years. |

| Tamil Years. | Equal to A.D. | | D. N. V. T. | |
|---|---|---|---|---|
| 2... | 79 | March ... | 14 42 23 45 | Piramathi. |
| | | | 15 31 15 | deduction for a common year. |
| 1... | 78 | March ... | 14 26 52 30 | Vekuthaniya. |

The meaning of the last expression is that the first year of the *Salivakana Sakaptham* corresponds with *Vekuthaniya*, the 12th year of the cycle, and that it commenced on the 15th of March A.D. 78 at 26 N. 52 V. 30 T. that is, reckoning the 15th to have commenced at midnight, as Europeans usually reckon their day.

18. To find the beginning of a given month. Take for instance the Saka year 1801; its beginning is:

| | | D. N. V. T. | |
|---|---|---|---|
| A. D. 1878 April | ... | 11 4 22 30 | which is also the beginning of Siththirai. |
| Add | ... | 30 55 32 00 | the length of Siththirai. |
| | | 41 59 54 30 | |
| Deduct | ... | 30 00 00 00 | the number of days in April. |
| May | ... | 11 59 54 30 | beginning of Vaiyasi. |
| Add | ... | 31 24 12 00 | the length of Vaiyasi. |
| | | 43 24 6 30 | |
| Deduct | ... | 31 00 00 00 | the number of days in May. |
| June | ... | 12 24 6 30 | the beginning of Ani. |
| Add | ... | 31 36 38 00 | the length of Ani. |
| | | 44 00 44 30 | |
| Deduct | ... | 30 00 00 00 | the number of days in June. |

| | | D. | N. | V. | T. | |
|---|---|---|---|---|---|---|
| July | ... | 14 | 00 | 44 | 30 | the beginning of Adi. |
| Add | ... | 31 | 28 | 12 | 00 | the length of Adi. |
| | | 45 | 28 | 56 | 30 | |
| Deduct | ... | 31 | 00 | 00 | 00 | the number of days in July |
| August | ... | 14 | 28 | 56 | 30 | the beginning of Avani. |
| Add | ... | 31 | 2 | 10 | 00 | the length of Avani. |
| | | 45 | 31 | 6 | 30 | |
| Deduct | ... | 31 | 00 | 00 | 00 | the number of days in August. |
| September | ... | 14 | 31 | 6 | 30 | the beginning of Puraddasi. |
| Add | ... | 30 | 27 | 22 | 00 | the length of Puraddasi. |
| | | 44 | 58 | 28 | 30 | |
| Deduct | ... | 30 | 00 | 00 | 00 | the number of days in September |
| October | ... | 14 | 58 | 28 | 30 | the beginning of Atpasi. |
| Add | ... | 29 | 54 | 7 | 00 | the length of Atpasi. |
| | | 44 | 52 | 35 | 30 | |
| Deduct | ... | 31 | 00 | 00 | 00 | the number of days in October |
| November | ... | 13 | 52 | 35 | 30 | the beginning of Karththikai |
| Add | ... | 29 | 30 | 24 | 00 | the length of Karththikai. |
| | | 43 | 22 | 59 | 30 | |
| Deduct | ... | 30 | 00 | 00 | 00 | the number of days in November |
| December | ... | 13 | 22 | 59 | 30 | the beginning of Markali. |
| Add | ... | 29 | 20 | 53 | 00 | the length of Markali. |
| | | 42 | 43 | 52 | 30 | |
| Deduct | ... | 31 | 00 | 00 | 00 | the number of days in December |

| | | D. | N. | V. | T. | |
|---|---|---|---|---|---|---|
| A.D. 1879, January | ... | 11 | 43 | 52 | 30 | the beginning of Thai. |
| Add | ... | 29 | 27 | 16 | 00 | the length of Thai. |
| | | 41 | 11 | 8 | 30 | |
| Deduct | ... | 31 | 00 | 00 | 00 | the number of days in January |
| February | ... | 10 | 11 | 8 | 30 | the beginning of Mási. |
| Add | ... | 29 | 48 | 24 | 00 | the length of Mási. |
| | | 39 | 59 | 32 | 30 | |
| Deduct | ... | 28 | 00 | 00 | 00 | this is a common year, & Feb-[ruary has only 28 days. |
| March | ... | 11 | 59 | 32 | 30 | the beginning of Paingkuni. |
| | | 30 | 20 | 21 | 15 | the length of Paingkuni. |
| | | 42 | 19 | 53 | 45 | |
| Deduct | ... | 31 | 00 | 00 | 00 | the number of days in March. |
| April | ... | 11 | 19 | 53 | 45 | |

This is the beginning of a new *Siththirai*, *i. e.*, the first month of the *Saka* year 1802, whose cyclic name is *Piramathi*.

19. To mark the first date of the month.

The expression May 11 59 54 30 which occurs in connexion with *Vaikasi* of *Saka* 1801 means, as has already been explained, that the first date (not the actual beginning) of the month of *Vaikasi* is the 13th, and not the 11th of May, which stands next to the 59 *nadi*, 54 *vinadi*, and 30 *thatparai*. For, the expression May 11 59 54 30 means that 11 days, 59 *nadi*, 54 *vinadi*, and 30 *thatparai* are fully past in May when *Vaikasi* begins. Accordingly, the 11th of May is wholly past, and 59 *nadi*, 54 *vinadi* and 30 *thatparai* are also past in the 12th of May. This brings us to the night of the 12th of May, that is, to 5 *vinadi* and 30 *thatparai* before the 13th of May commences according to the European way of reckoning days.

Now, it is a rule of the common *Pagnchangkam* that when a month begins between sunset and sunrise the first date of that month is the day which begins with the sunrise that follows the true beginning of the month. And it must be borne in mind that this takes place, so far only as the reckoning of the *dates* of the month are concerned. In Tamil treatises this same rule will be found stated in slightly different words, thus,—"When the beginning of a month falls after the sun has gone down, the day which commences at the next sunrise, is the first date of the month."

The difference between the two modes of expression is due to the fact that the Tamil day is reckoned from sunrise to sunrise, while the European day is from midnight to midnight.

20. To test the accuracy of future calculations, the following rules will be of great assistance.

1st.—In 576 years the fraction 15 N. 31 V. 15 T., which occurs in the length of the year, amounts to 149 whole days. Hence at every interval of 576 years, the year will begin at the same hour of the day.

As for instance:

D. N. V. T.
The beginning of Saka 1801, being equal to A. D. 1878 Apr. 11 4 22 30
By deducting... ... 576 on both sides and making allowance for
—— intercalary days.

D. N. V. T.
We have the beginning of Saka 1225, equal to A. D. 1302 Mar. 25 4 22 30
Again deduct ... ... ... 576 on both sides and allow intercalary
—— days.

D. N. V. T.
We have the beginning of Saka 649, equal to A. D. 726 Mar. 20 4 22 30
Again deduct ... ... ... 576 on both sides and allow intercalary
—— days.

D. N. V. T.
And we have the beginning of Saka 73, equal to A.D. 150 Mar. 15 4 22 30

2nd.—*Saka* year 1 being equal to A.D. 78 March 14 D. 26 N. 52 V. 30 T., it will be found that *Saka* 151 is equal to A.D. 228 March 15 D. 15 N. 0 V. 0 T., which means that the *Saka* year 151 began at sunrise *after* the 15th (*i. e.*, *on* the 16th) of March A.D. 228. In like mannor:

| | | D. | N. | V. | T. | |
|---|---|---|---|---|---|---|
| Saka 727 is equal to A.D. 804 | March | 20 | 15 | 0 | 0, | and |
| Saka 1303 to A.D. 138 ............ | March | 25 | 15 | 0 | 0, | and |
| Saka 1879 to A.D. 1956.............. | April | 12 | 15 | 0 | 0 | |

21. The whole of the above results have been obtainéd by a process of supputation by recession, taking the *Pagnchangkam* for the year *Isura* as our basis. The same results may be obtained by direct calculation from *Saka* 1 as soon as that has been found to correspond with A.D. 78 March 14 D. 26 N. 52 V. 30 T.

As for instance:

| Saka | A.D. | | | | | | |
|---|---|---|---|---|---|---|---|
| Saka 1= | A. D. 78 | March | 14 | 26 | 52 | 30 | Veku'hániya. |
| 480 | 480 | | 4 | 10 | 00 | 00 | addition for 480 years. |
| 481 | 458 | March | 18 | 36 | 52 | 30 | Vekuthániya. |
| 20 | 20 | | 00 | 10 | 25 | 00 | addition for 20 years. |
| 501 | 578 | March | 18 | 47 | 17 | 30 | Vilampi. |
| 8 | 8 | | 00 | 4 | 10 | 00 | addition for 8 years, |
| 509 | 586 | March | 18 | 51 | 27 | 30 | Parpava, |
| 1 | 1 | | 00 | 15 | 31 | 15 | addition for a common year. |
| 510 | 510 | March | 19 | 6 | 58 | 45 | Pi avangka, |
| 1 | 1 | | 00 | 15 | 31 | 15 | addition for a common year. |
| 511 | 588 | March | 19 | 22 | 30 | 00 | Kílaka. |
| 1 | 1 | | 00 | 44 | 28 | 45 | deduction for a leap year. |
| 512 | 589 | March | 18 | 38 | 1 | 15 | Saumiya. |

Or the same result may be briefly obtained by taking the nearest known year for a basis, as for instance, *Saka* 73 may be found from *Saka* 50.

| | | | | | | | |
|---|---|---|---|---|---|---|---|
| Saka 50=A. D. | 127 | March | 15 | 7 | 23 | 45 | Pirapava. |
| | | | 00 | 10 | 25 | 00 | addition for 20 years. |
| 70= | 147 | March | 15 | 17 | 48 | 45 | |
| | | | 00 | 13 | 26 | 15 | deduction for a leap year and 2 common years. |
| 73= | 150 | March | 15 | 4 | 22 | 30 | |

22. *Ullamudaiyan* and other authorities lay down independant rules to calculate the year and its various astrological parts. For example. To find the *Saka* year 512, take the previous year 511, add to it 3179 being the number of years that had expired in the *Kaliyuga* before the *Sakaptham* commenced, and multiply the sum (3,690) by $\frac{210389}{576}$ the length of the Tamil year, subtract $\frac{1237}{576}$ being a correction of 2 days, 8 *nalikai*, 57 *vinadi* and 15 *thatparai* for the epoch. The result will give the commencement of the required year.

Thus $511+3179=3690$

$$3690\times\frac{210389}{576}=\frac{776335410}{576}$$

$$\frac{776335410-1237}{576}=\frac{776334173}{576}$$

$\frac{776334173}{576}$ = 1347802 days 23 n. 1 v. 15 t. which is the commencement of Saka year 512.

But on reference to our previous calculation we find that the commencement of 512 *Saka* is marked 38 N. 1 V. 15 T. instead of 23 N., 1 V., 15 T. This difference is accounted for by the fact that our mode of calculation assumes the day to commence at 12 o'clock in the night, while *Ullamudaiyan's* day does not commence till sunrise. The difference between midnight and sunrise being (roughly speaking) 15 N., it accounts for the discrepency.

23. From the above may also be deduced the day of the week in which the year commences. Divide 1,347,802 (which represents the member of days passed since the beginning of *Kaliyukam*) by seven, (the number of days in the week) the remainder will shew the day of the week. Here the remainder is 1, shewing that 192,543 full weeks and 1 day have passed and as the *Kaliyukam* commenced on a Friday, the 1 indicates that the year 512 commenced on a Saturday which is accordingly reckoned as the first day of the month of *Siththirai* or *medam* (Aries). To 1 D. 23 N. 1 V. 15 T. add 2 D. 55 N. 32 V. (which is the *Sankirama Vakkiyam* for the next month) and the sum 4 D. 18 N. 33 V. 15 T. shews that the month of *Vaikasi* or *Idapam* (Taurus) begins at 18. N. 33 V. 15 T after the 4th day of the *Kaliyuka week i. e.* on a Tuesday. And the 10th of that month would be a Thursday, and so on.

To find the day of the week in which the year 513 commences. To 1 D. 23 N. 1 V. 15 T. add 1 D. 15 N. 31 V. 15 T. (*i. e.* a year, omitting the full weeks) the sum 2 D. 38 N. 32 V. 30 T. gives the answer to be a Sunday. To find the beginning of the next month, add to this the *Sangkirama Vakyam* 2 D, 55 N. 32 V. the sum 5 D. 34 N. 4 V. 30 T. makes the day Wednesday. And the 10th would be a Friday.

By a *Sangkirama Vakkiyam* is understood the addition that must be made to the end of each month to obtain the day of the week in which the succeeding month begins. And this is obtained from the lengths of the months by casting out the weeks.

24. Before closing the subject we shall give another example of the manner of finding Tamil years according to

native authorities (see "Oriental Astronomer," Jaffna 1848, by H. R. Hoisington.)

To find the begining of 1801 Saka.

| | |
|---|---|
| Take the previous year ... ... .. | 1800 |
| Add ... ... ... ... ... ... ... | 3179 |
| Total... | 4979 |

Multiply 4979 by $\frac{210389}{576}$

From the product $\frac{1047526831}{576}$ deduct $\frac{1237}{576}$

The remainder $\frac{1047525594}{576}$ = 1818620 days 49 n. 22 v. 30 t. exactly.

It must be borne in mind that the 49 N. are here reckoned from sunrise. It will therefore be 4 N. after midnight which corresponds with what has been given elsewhere as the commencement of this year.

To find the day of the week in which the Saka year 1801 commences Divide 1,818,620 days by 7. And the remainder 6 indicates the day to be a Thursday. But 49 N, on a Tamil Thursday will be 4 N. A.M. on Friday according to European reckoning. In the *Pagnohangkam* the first date will be found marked as Friday, but for quite a different reason namely, for the rule given elsewhere that when a month begins during sunset and sunrise the first date of that month is reckoned as commencing at the following sunrise although for astrological purposes the commencement of the month is exactly the hour, minute and second at which it occurred.

To find the commencement of Vaikasi.

| | D. | N | V. | T. | |
|---|---|---|---|---|---|
| To ... | 6 | 49 | 22 | 30 | |
| Add ... | 30 | 55 | 32 | 00 | the length of Vaikasi. |
| From the total... | 37 | 44 | 54 | 30, | |

by casting out whole weeks we have 2 D. 44 N. 54 V. 30 T. which indicates that the month commenced on a Tamil Sunday at 44 N, &c.

Similarly the remaining months may be found.

25. To find the date, month, and year of the A.D. era, with which the commencement of *Saka* 1801 corresponds proceed as follows.

As there are in a Tamil year 365 D., 15 N., 31 V., 15 T.

And as 1800 years have expired in the *Sakaptham*,

Multiply 365 D., 15 N., 31 V., 15 T. by 1800 and the product is 657465 D., 37 N., 30 V.

Again as the *Sakaptham* commenced at A.D., 78, March 14 D., 26 N., 52 V., 30 T

Find the number of days that had expired in the A.D. era before the *Sakaptham* thus.

Multiply 365 the length of the European year by 77 the number of full A.D. years that had expired before *Sakaptham*.

The product is 28015 days

To this add... ......19 the number of intercalary days which occurred during the 77 years.

Also..........73 number of full days that have expired in January, February, and a part of March 78 A.D.

| | D. | N. | V. | T. | |
|---|---|---|---|---|---|
| Also............... | 00 | 26 | 52 | 30 | the fraction of day that had expired out of the 15th of March. |
| Total... | 28197 | 26 | 52 | 30 | |
| Add to this the first product | 657465 | 37 | 30 | 0 | |

And the sum 685,663 D. 4 N. 22 V. 30 T, represents the time passed from the beginning of the A.D. era to the end of the *Saka* year 1800

During this period there have been 1877 European full years of 365 days each, giving a total of ... ... ... 685105 days.

| | |
|---|---|
| Add to this 468 intercalary days, recollecting that the year A. D. 1800 was a common year. | 468 |
| Total... | 685573 |
| From this take away the 11 days by which A. D. 1752 was short | 11 |
| | 685562 days. |

| | D. | N. | V. | T. |
|---|---|---|---|---|
| Now from the sum | 685663 | 4 | 22 | 30 |
| Take away ... | 685562 | 0 | 0 | 0 |
| The difference is | 101 | 4 | 22 | 30 |

This difference shews the number of days that have expired in the year A.D., 1878.

In January, February and March of 1878 A.D., there were 90 days which when deducted from 101 leave a difference of 11 days.

Hence the year *Saka* 1801 commenced in A.D., 1878 April 11 D., 4 N, 22 V., 30 T.

It is again worth repeating that 11 D., 4 N., 22 V, 30 T., represent the time that has already fully and completely passed in April, and that the days meant in this expression are European days *i. e.*, days which are reckoned from midnight to midnight.

THE END OF APPENDIX.

# A GLOSSARY OF FOREIGN WORDS CONTAINED IN THE VAIPAVA-MALAI.

*Achari, Achariya...Achariyar* (honorific)...a priest.

*Adchaya*...See Pagnchangkam,p.lxxxix.

*Adi*...See Pagnchangkam,p.lxxxix.

*Akkiraram, Akkiraharam*...residence for priests.

*Alayam*...temple

*Amirtha*...Ambrosia,nectar.

*Amral*,p.xxxv.

*Ani*...See Pagnchangkam,pp.lxxxix.

*Anthirasu*, Andirado,p.xxxv.

*Anuradhapura*...A city built by Anuradho one of Wijayo companions, on the Kadamba River. Mahawanso p.50.

*Athikari, Adigar*...minister.

*Banga*...Wango or Bengal.

*Batticaloa*...A fief of the Kingdom of Kandi held by one of the chiefs of the Wannis. The Portuguese took possession of it in 1622 and built the fort in 1627, but their power never extended beyond Puliantivu. In 1638 the Dutch Admiral from Batavia took it. Tennent II. 466-484. In 1672 the Dutch abandoned the fort. Tennent II. p. 486

*Brahman*...See p. lxxxiii...The priestly caste.

*Chavakar*...Javas.

*Chera*...Sera,p. lii.

*Cheri*...A village inhabited by one caste of people.

*Chilaw*...Salabham of the Tamils, being a corruption of the Sanscrit "Jalevaha" (diving for pearls). It was wrested by the Tamils from the King of Ceylon in the 14th century. It was occupied in turn by the Moors, Portuguese and Dutch, from the last of whom it was taken by the English in 1796. Tennent II. p. 629.

*Chola, Sola*, p.liii.

*Dona Catharina...* App. p. lxxviii.

*Imayamalai*...Himalaya mountains.

*Indra*...See *Inthiran.*

*Inthiran*...King of the gods...*Inthirani*, his wife.

*Inthiresu*...English.

*Iramanthapuram*...Ramnad.

*Irappramathu Saththiya Vetham*...The Reformed True Religion i.e., Protes tantism.

*Ithikasa*...This word is usually found coupled with *puranam*, thus: Ithi kasa-puranangkal, which means *ithikasams*, and *puranams*. The difference between an *ithikasam* and a *puranam* is not well defined. The term ithikasam is generally applied to the two heroic histories *Maha Bharata* and *Ramayana.*

*Puranam* may be defined to be accounts of gods and *rishis*. There are 18 principal *puranams* and as many secondary *puranams* ( called *upapuranams*) besides a host of Sthala-puranams. Sthalapu ranams are those written in praise of sacred places.

*Kachchakkathiththa*..Kachchai-thurai, or Kasaththurai in the Peninsula of Jaffna. Also another place which was nine yojanas from Anuradha pura. Mahawanso p. 139.

*Kadat-koddai*...Fort Hammanheil at Kaits.

*Kalavuththi*...See Pagnchangkam,p. lxxxix.

*Kanthalai*...Gantalawe or Dantalawe is according to Singhalese historians a work of King Maha Sen whose reign terminated A.D. 301. Major

Forbes II. p 38. But the Tamils ascribe its origin to Kulukkoddan. App. xlii-xliv.

*Kanya kumari* or *Kanniya kumari*...Cape Comorin.

*Kara*...See Pagnchangam, p. lxxxix.

*Kashi*...Benares.

*Kathirmalai*.. A Tamil name of Anuradhapura. This is not the same place as Kathirgamam or Kattragama (Kachcharagama) with which it is generally confounded. The original site of Kathiramalai or Katiragiri is in the Bintenne District of the Eastern Province situated between the Mahavelliganga and the Maduru Oya, near the borders of the present North-Central Province.

*Kayilai*...*Kayilasam*...Residence of Siva.

*Ketheram*...See Kasi Kandam. App p. xxv.

*Kshattriya*...See Kshatri, p. lxxxiii...The military caste.

*Kottiar*...By Boschouwer's treaty the Dutch (A. D. 1612) obtained permission from the Emperor of Kandi to erect a fort. In 1675 they had constantly from 80 to 100 ships from Coromandel In 1672 the Dutch abandoned this fort. Tennent II. p. 38, 485.

*Kolumpu*...Colombo.

*Koyil*...Temple.

*Kulakkoddan*...*Kulakkoddu maharaja*. See Kalveddu App. pp. xxxix-xliv.

*Lada*...A sub-division of Maghada. Mahawanso, Int. p 42.

*Lala*...See Lada.

*Langka*...According to the author of the Tamil Ramayan this word is derived from a Sanscrit root containing the idea of inacessibility. App. p. ii.

*Maghada*...Behar.

*Magnchan*...Bed.

*Maharaja* Great king.

*Maka maka*...A festival which takes place once in twelve years.

*Manmatha*...See Pagnchangkam, p. lxxxix.

*Manmathan*...God of Love.

*Masi*...See Pagnchangkam, p. lxxxix.

*Mathurai*...Madura.

*Matkam*...Religion.

*Muni*...Sage.

*Nadu*...Country.

*Nathan*...God.

*Nayaki*...Goddess.

*Negombo*...The Portuguese were dispossessed of the fort of Negombo by tl Dntch in 1640, but they recovered it soon afterwards, and finally lost in 1644

*Pandaram*...A regligious mendicant.

*Pandi*...*Madura,* liii.

*Paramesvaran*...Siva

*Parangki*...Feringee...Portuguese.

*Parvathi*...Wife of Siva.

*Piragnchu*...French.

*Piramanan*...Brahman.

*Puranas*...See *Ithikasa*

*Puraddasi*...See Pagnchangkam lxxxix.

*Puruththikkal*...Portugal.

*Puthaththampi*...xxxv.

*Puvineya*...Bhuvaneka.

*Raja*...King.

*Rishi*...Sage.

*Rakshasas*...See Iradchathar. App. pp. i-xxi.

*Ramanathapuram*...Ramnad.

*Salivakana Sakaptham*...See Pagnchangkam, p. lxxxix.

*Santhachchaivu* . Chandrachano App. p. lxxiv.

*Saththiya Vetham*...True Religion, Roman Catholicism.

*Saka*...*Sakaptham*...Pagnchangkam, p. lxxxix.

*Sappira magncham*...A high bed on legs, with a canopy over it.

*Savakar*...Javas.

*Saveriyar*...Xavier.

*Sengkadakanakari*...p. lxxiv.

*Sera*...See Chera.

*Singha bahu*...App. lvii.

*Singhalese*...See pp. xlvii-lxxxi.

*Saivite*...A follower of Siva.

*Siva*...*Shiva*...*Sivan*...One of the hindu triad.

*Sola*...See Chola.

*Sonakar*...See Moors, p. lxxxii.

*Supakiruthu*...See Pagnchangkam, p. lxxxix.

*Tamils*, pp. xlvii-lxxxi.

*Tammanna*...See Thammanna.

*Thai*...See Pagnchangkam, lxxxix.

*Thampalakamam*...Tambalgam.

*Thammanna*. p. xlix.

*Tharangkampadi*...Tranquebar.

*Then-nadu*...*Thenthesam*...Southern extremity of India.

*Thenmarkar*...People of Denmark, Danes.

*Thirikonamalai*...See Trincomalie.

*Trincomalie*...The Portuguese took it in 1622, demolished the temple of Siva. Some of the idols were rescued and conveyed to the pagoda of Tamblegam. Tennent II. 484. The French took it in 1672 but abandoned it for want of provisions. Tennent II. 485. They renewed their attempt in 1782 and took possession of it, but in the following year it was restored to the Dutch, by whom it was held till the capture of Ceylon by Great Britain in 1795.

*Ulanthes*...Hollanders, Dutch.

*Ukkirasinghan*, p. xxxi.

*Urkavat-turai*...Kayts or Kaits.

*Vaddukkodai*...Batticotta.

*Vaipavamalai*...A historical garland.

*Vaku*...The same as *Baku*.

*Vanni*...Two derivations are assigned to this name. That signifying the "forest" which covers it to a great extent is probably the true one. This region is the extreme northern section of the island immediately adjoining the peninsula of Jaffna and in the time of the Dutch its southern boundaries were the Aripo River and the Kalu-aar.

In modern times the Vannis were governed by native princes who paid tribute to the Rajas of Jaffna and later still to the kings of Kandi. After the capture of Jaffna, the Portuguese and the Dutch became the nominal sovereigns of the Vannis. But they exercised no control over the inhabitants, who made sudden descents on the cultivated lands on either seaborde of the island, and carried on a predatory warfare at Mannar and Trincomalie.

In 1803 Panda Vannian of Newera-Kalavia district undertook to expel the English from the country and succeeded in occupying Cottiar. He drove out the garrison at Mullattivu. But he was speedily overcome.

One of the last descendants of the Vanniyar was an old lady who resided in 1848 near the fort of Jaffna. Tennent II. 508, 509, 510.

*Vanniyar*...See Vanni.

*Vaya*...The author of an ancient work on the history of Jaffna—not extant now.

*Vedar*...The same as the Singhalese "Veddhas" which is evidently a cor ruption of the Tamil word "Vedar" who were scarcely allowed to be human beings, p. viii.

*Vedaratta*...Bintenne, a vast expanse to the N. E. of the Kandyan mountains. Tennent II. 408. It is about 90 miles in length by half that breadth, is situated in the south eastern section of the Island and extends towards the sea, from the base of Badulla and the Uvah hills. Tennent II. 437.

*Velalar*... *Vellalar*...Cultivator caste, i. e., same as Vasiya, p. lxxxiii.

*Vibhishana*. App. pp. ii-iii.

*Vijaya-kumara*...Vijayo or Vijaya, ix--xiii, xliv.

*Vijayo*...See Vijaya-kumara.

*Vilampi*...See Pagnchangkam, p. lxxxix.

*Vimala-tharuma*...Wimala Dharma.

*Virarakavan*, p. lxxxv.

*Vishnu*...One of the hindu triad.

*Yavakar*...Javas, Malays.

*Yojana*...16 English miles.

*Yugas*...See Pagnchangkam, App. lxxxix.

NOTE. The pages indicated in Roman numerals refer to the Appendix.

The references to the Mahawanso, Rajavali and Rajaratnacari found in the Appendix apply to the English translations of those works now in use in the Island.